MONEY

Ancient Italian bronze coin of the city of Hatra, 3rd century B.C.

Bolivian gold 8-scudos coin, 1841

Indian gold "pagodas," 17th–19th century

Australian cupro-nickel 50 cents, 1970

Indian gold mohur, 17th century

GOVERNMENT OF CEYLON
THE
THIS NOTE IS LEGAL TENDER FOR THE PAYMENT
OF AN AMOUNT NOT EXCEEDING FIVE RUPEES
TEN CENTS
TEN CENTS
14TH JULY 1942
COMMISSIONERS OF CURRENCY

Ceylon (Sri Lanka) 10-cent note, 1942

10

LE CONTREFACTEUR SERA PUNI DES TRAVAUX FORCÉS À PERPÉTUITÉ.

Djibouti French colonial note, 20th century

Ancient Roman medals showing minting (below) and banking (right)

Ancient Greek silver coin showing Alexander the Great, 4th century B.C.

Moroccan bronze coins, unseparated as taken from the mold, 19th century

Spanish silver "piece of eight" reales from Mexico, 1732

VTRAQUE VNUM

1732

Gold 10-ducat coin of Transylvania, 17th century

EYEWITNESS BOOKS

MONEY

USSR cupro-nickel ruble, 1967

Written by
JOE CRIBB

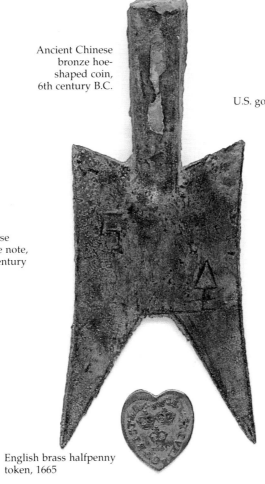

Ancient Chinese bronze hoe-shaped coin, 6th century B.C.

U.S. gold "eagle," 1797

Siamese paper money, 1860s

Japanese Temple note, 19th century

English brass halfpenny token, 1665

Stoddart

Zambian bronze penny, 1966

English gold sovereign (1901) and brass sovereign balance

Ancient Greek silver: broken coin, cut ingot, and wire from Tarento (Italy) hoard

Ancient Roman silver coin, 3rd century B.C.

Ancient Indian gold coin, 1st century A.D.

Australian aluminium-bronze 2-dollar coin, 1988

Ottoman Turkish gold zeri-mahbub, 18th century

Ancient Roman gold bar made from melted down coins, 4th century

Ancient Chinese bronze knife-shaped coin, 3rd century B.C.

Persian silver wire "larin" coin, 16th century

This Eyewitness Book has been conceived by Dorling Kindersley Limited and Editions Gallimard

Project Editor Linda Martin
Art Editor Richard Czapnik
Senior Editor Sophie Mitchell
Senior Art Editor Julia Harris
Editorial Director Sue Unstead
Art Director Anne-Marie Bulat
Special photography Chas Howson,
Department of Coins and Medals, The British Museum

First published in Canada in 1990 by
STODDART PUBLISHING CO. LIMITED
34 Lesmill Road, Toronto, Canada M3B 2T6

Canadian Cataloguing in Publication Data
Cribb, Joe
Money
(Eyewitness books)
ISBN 0-7737-2345-5
1. Money - Juvenile literature.
I. Howson, Chas. II. Title. III. Series.
HG221.5.C75 1990   j332.4   C89-095498-4

Color reproduction by Colourscan, Singapore
Typeset by Windsorgraphics, Ringwood, Hampshire
Printed in Italy by A. Mondadori Editore, Verona

Tonga cupro-nickel 1-pa'anga coin, 1977

Contents

Indian cupro-nickel
10-paise coin, 1964

Chinese silver good-luck coin
charm, 19th century

This is money

IT IS DIFFICULT TO IMAGINE a world without money; every country has its own, and its history reaches back to the earliest written records of human activity. But what exactly is money? Money can be many different things: for most people it is coins, banknotes, plastic cards, and savings in the bank. But for some people in the not too distant past, it has been feathers, stones, beads, and shells (pp. 8-9), for these were the objects they considered valuable. What allows us to describe all these things with the same word, "money," is that they are all an acceptable and recognized means of payment. This even applies to the money you cannot see or feel – the money that is stored in bank computer records, and which can be spent in the same way as the coins and notes in your pocket.

TODAY'S MONEY
Banknotes, coins, and plastic cards come in various shapes, sizes, and colors, but they are all called money because they are all used to buy goods or services.

The earliest money

It is not known exactly when money was first used. The oldest written records of it are from ancient Mesopotamia (now in southern Iraq) about 4,500 years ago. Ancient Mesopotamian cuneiform (wedge-shaped) inscriptions describe payments being made with weighed amounts of silver. Since then, weighed amounts of metal have been used as money in many parts of the world, and this practice led to the invention of coins (pp. 10–11).

MESOPOTAMIAN MONEY
The inscription on this tablet commemorates "prices" during the reign of Sin-Kasid of Uruk (1865–1804 B.C.): "In the course of his reign, one shekel [a unit of weight] of silver on the local standard could buy three measures of barley, twelve mina of wool, ten mina of bronze, or three measures of sesame oil, according to the price in his kingdom."

HAMMURABI'S LAWS
This big stone column shows a god giving Hammurabi, king of Babylonia (1792–1750 B.C.), laws referring to how silver should be used. Law 204 says: "If a common man slaps the face of another common man, he must pay ten shekels of silver as compensation."

GOOSE WEIGHT
So that silver and other goods could be weighed accurately, the ancient Mesopotamians had made official weights. This example weighs about 30 shekels. There were 60 shekels in a mina.

Ten

Twelve

Wool

Barley

Bronze

CUNEIFORM
By deciphering cuneiform script, scientists have discovered many different ways in which weighed amounts of silver were used as money in ancient Mesopotamia. The characters above appear in the inscription on the tablet.

EGYPTIAN WALL-PAINTING
This ancient Egyptian wall-painting (14th century B.C.), found in a tomb at Thebes, shows gold rings being weighed on a balance. The Egyptians used balances and weights to measure the value of precious metals.

Lump of gold

STONE WEIGHT
The hieroglyphic inscription on this small Egyptian stone weight is faint, but it tells us that the weight was used for weighing gold. A clearer version of the hieroglyph for "gold" can be seen on the Egyptian gold coin on p. 54.

EGYPTIAN HOARD
The ancient Egyptians also developed a money system using weighed amounts of metal; records exist of gold, silver, and copper being weighed out as payments. Because the weight set its value, the shape and size of the metal was unimportant. The money was as varied in shape as the bars, rings, and lumps of silver in this 14th-century-B.C. hoard from el-Amarna.

Silver in this form was very convenient as it was easy to cut into smaller bits

Position of string on the scale showed how much the silver in the pan weighed

Ivory rod marked with scale

Heavy silver bar

IN THE BALANCE
Although the Chinese had been making coins since the 6th century B.C. (p. 11), they had never made them out of gold and silver. Official balance weights were made, but until the 1930s traders still measured amounts of gold and silver for everyday business on small hand-balances like this one. The silver ingots were made in special shapes to show where they came from. The ingots below are all from northeast China, and were made in the 19th century.

Brass counterweight was moved along the scale until the ivory rod hung level

Burmese weight made of bronze

The largest ingot weighs one liang (ounce), and the smallest one weighs one-tenth of one liang. Ingots as heavy as 50 liang were also used.

Flower pattern

"FLOWER SILVER"
The only official money in 18th-century Burma was weighed amounts of silver. Most of the silver was poured out into pancake-shaped disks known as "flower silver." The name refers to the patterns on the silver, which were made by blowing through a pipe at the metal as it set.

LION WEIGHT
All the official Burmese weights, like this one, were in the form of animals such as elephants, ducks, bulls, and lions. A star-shaped mark was stamped on the base of each weight to show that it had been checked by the king's official.

Funny money?

As HEAVY AS STONE, as light as a feather, "money" comes in many forms. The objects on these pages may seem very curious, but they were not strange to the people who used them. In some tribal societies, objects that had a recognized value were counted out and used for payments: ornaments such as shells; tools such as hoes; foodstuffs such as salt and grain; and cloth (pp. 54–55). As with our money today, and the weighed metal money of ancient Mesopotamia (p. 6), tribal societies had very strict rules about the value and payment of their money; it was generally used to pay fines and settle social obligations, such as marriage and compensation payments.

MEXICAN MONEY AXE
When the Spanish conquistadors entered Mexico (p. 39), the Mexicans were using cacao (chocolate) beans and small copper axes in payments. The money axes were too fragile to be used as tools!

SUDANESE MONEY HOE
There are many reports of iron hoes being used in 19th-century Africa to make payments in wedding settlements. The ancient Chinese also made payments with hoes.

STONE MONEY
The stone below is a *small* example of the stone disks used by the people of Yap, an island in the Pacific Ocean, to make social payments and settle disputes. The largest examples measured up to 12 ft (4 m) across!

Stone is made of aragonite, a form of limestone

Reed binding to prevent breakage

Herd of African cattle

ETHIOPIAN SALT BAR
Bars of rock salt were widely used both for cooking and as money in Ethiopia until the 1920s. The bars were bound in reeds to prevent breakage. Elsewhere in eastern Africa, herds of cattle are still considered symbols of wealth and status.

MONEY COWRIE SHELLS
The earliest reports of payments with cowrie shells were from China about 3,500 years ago. When the Chinese writing system was being developed, the cowrie shell was thought the best symbol for money (right). Cowrie shells were also used in 10th- to 18th-century India, l7th-century Thailand, and l9th-century Africa.

Treasure

To sell

To buy

To barter

Cowrie shell symbol

NIGERIAN COPPER MANILLA
Copper rings, known as manillas, were used to make payments in West Africa as early as the 15th century. They were still being used until l948 (p. 54) among the Ibo people of eastern Nigeria.

Cowrie-shell decoration

Beads made from clam shells

FEATHER MONEY
This "money" was made from tiny red feathers glued together and tied to vegetable-fiber coils that could be up to 32 ft (10 m) long. They were used by the Pacific islanders of Santa Cruz as payments at marriage ceremonies and to acquire ocean-going canoes. The brighter the feathers, the more valuable the coil.

Square design may represent an Indian village

Salt bar

WAMPUM
This belt of beads, called wampum, was made from white and purple clam shells by North American Indians. Early European settlers told how the Indians used the beads as money, usually to settle agreements between villages. Wampum belts often had designs worked into them; each of the three "squares" on this belt may have represented a different Indian village.

The first coins

COINING TOOLS
Roman coin showing ancient tools for making coins: punch (top), anvil (center), hammer (right), and tongs (left).

Coins are pieces of metal marked with a design that instantly shows that they are money. The earliest known coins were made during the 7th century B.C. in the kingdom of Lydia (in the country we now call Turkey). Weighed lumps of electrum (a mixture of gold and silver) were used by the Lydians as money, and were stamped with pictures to confirm their weight and therefore their value in payments. This process of stamping is called "minting." The shape of the coins was unimportant. The stamp on the coin was a personal seal that identified the person who had guaranteed the coin's weight; the Lydian kings stamped their coins with a lion's head. This new method of organizing money was a great success and soon spread into Europe. Although the Lydian invention was the first, the same idea was developed elsewhere to standardize other forms of metal money: copper lumps in Italy and southern Russia, bronze tools and shells in China, silver rings in Thailand, and gold and silver bars in Japan.

Mark made by punches

One-stater coins

1/6-stater coins

1/24-stater coin

LYDIAN ELECTRUM COINS
The weight of Lydian money was measured in units called "staters," about 1/2 oz (14 g) each. Fractional coins were also made; coins as small as 1/96 stater were made! Each metal lump was placed on an anvil, and the punches were pushed into the lump with a hammer. Because the anvil had been engraved with the lion's head emblem of the Lydian kings, these coins (600 B.C.) now had this image stamped on them.

Caria, c. 530 B.C.

Andros, c. 525 B.C.

Ceos, c. 525 B.C.

Aegina, c. 540 B.C.

Athens, c. 540 B.C.

EARLY SILVER COINS
The idea of using coins as money spread from western Turkey into the Greek world. Within 100 years, coins were issued as far away as Italy and Libya. The pictures on four of these coins were the emblems of the place of issue: a lion for Caria in Turkey; a vase, a squid, and a turtle for the Aegean islands of Andros, Ceos, and Aegina. The beetle is the emblem of an Athenian official. The dates are known because the coins were found buried in the foundations of the temple of Artemis (right), the goddess of the hunt, built at Ephesus around 560 B.C.

Greek letters

Marked ingot made of copper

PERSONAL SEALS
On this coin from western Turkey (left), the Greek letters mean "I am the seal of Phanes." The design is similar to the Greek seal (above) which names its owner, Mandronax.

Knife-shaped coin

Olbian dolphin coins,
4th century B.C.

Hoe-
shaped coin

Olbian round coin,
4th century B.C.

CAST COPPER COINS
Before coinage was
adopted in Olbia
(Russia), Rome, and
other Latin and
Etruscan (pre-
Roman) cities of
central Italy, weighed
pieces of cast copper
were used as money.
Under the influence of
Greek coins, designs were
added to these copper ingots
(pieces of cast metal made in a
mold) to turn them into coins. In Olbia, most
of the cast copper pieces were round, but some
were cast in the shape of a dolphin, probably
because Olbia was on the Black Sea coast.

Cowrie-shell-
shaped coin

CHINESE TOOL AND SHELL COINS
The earliest Chinese coins (about
500 B.C.) were made from bronze in the
shape of the tools and cowrie shells that
had previously been used as money by the
Chinese. The tool-shaped coins were too
fragile to be used as actual tools!

ELEPHANT-SIZED COIN!
In Rome, the earliest marked
ingots kept the rectangular
shape used for unmarked
ingots. The Indian elephant
shown here is a reference to the
elephants used by a Greek
army that invaded southern
Italy in 280 B.C.

JAPANESE SHOGUN
Shoguns were
fearsome military
dictators who
ruled Japan
from the 12th to
the 19th century.

Gold coin,
1601

THAI RING-COINS
Before they made coins, the
people of Thailand used weighed silver
rings as money. When the rings were made
into coins in the 17th century, their shape
was changed by bending or hammering.
They were then stamped with official marks.

JAPANESE INGOT COINS
During the late 16th and early
17th centuries, the Japanese
leader Ieyasu, who became
the first Tokugawa Shogun
in 1603, reorganized Japan's
monetary system (p. 52). His
gold and silver
coins were in
the form of
hammered or
cast slabs, like
the ingots
previously
used as money.

Silver coin,
1601

Gold coin, 1818

11

The first paper money

Banknotes are only pieces of paper, yet they are accepted as money because it is what they *represent* that is valuable. It was the Chinese who first saw the advantages of handling money in the form of printed paper documents. During the 10th century, the Chinese government issued heavy iron coins that had little value. People started to leave their coins with merchants and to use the handwritten receipts the merchants gave them instead. In the early 11th century, the government took over from the merchants and printed receipts that could be used officially as money, and to make the system simpler, the receipts were given fixed values.

DIFFICULT TO LOSE!
It must have been very awkward to carry the banknote below. It measured 9 x 13 in (23 x 33 cm), the largest note ever issued.

JAPANESE NOTE
The idea of paper money spread to Japan during the 17th century. Most Japanese notes were issued by feudal clans and temples.

Japanese "bookmark" note of 1746

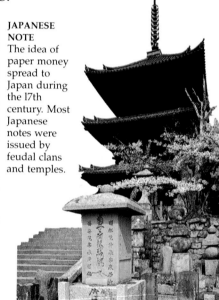

TEMPLE MONEY
Japanese temples – like this one in Kyoto – acted like banks, issuing their own paper money.

CHINESE PAPER MONEY
In the center of the design of this 14th-century Chinese note, you can just see the 1,000 coins it represented. The coins would have weighed about 8 lb (3.5 kg). It is not surprising that the Chinese were the first to use paper money!

ENGLISH MONEY ORDER
Before official printed banknotes appeared in Europe, handwritten paper "money" was used. This note (1665) was addressed by a John Lewis to the London money lenders Morriss and Clayton, asking them to pay 50 pounds of his money to his servant.

SWEDISH BANKNOTE
In 1661, during a coin shortage, the Swedish Stockholm Bank began to issue Europe's first printed paper money. This note (1666) represented 100 dalers (pp. 44–45).

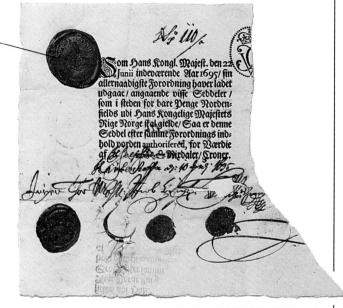

Wax seal

BANK OF SCOTLAND NOTE
During the late 17th century, printed paper money began to be issued in Britain. The Bank of Scotland issued notes valued in Scottish money, like this one dated 1723. Twelve Scottish pounds were equal to one English pound.

JOHN LAW
John Law (1671–1729) was a Scottish financier who lived in France.

NORWEGIAN MERCHANT'S NOTE
Following the Swedish example, a Norwegian merchant, Jorgen Thor Mohlen, issued printed notes for circulation as money (1695). Mohlen used the coins exchanged for the notes to fund his business.

FRENCH ROYAL BANKNOTE
It was Scotsman John Law who introduced the idea of printed paper money to France. In 1718 the bank that he had set up in Paris received the French king's approval to issue notes valued in silver coin. However, the bank issued too many notes, and they became worthless.

ITALIAN PAPAL NOTE
This 31-scudi note from the Bank of the Holy Spirit at Rome was issued in 1786, during the reign of Pope Pius VI, for circulation in the Papal States (ruled by the popes). The bank, set up by Pope Paul V in 1605, was Europe's first national bank.

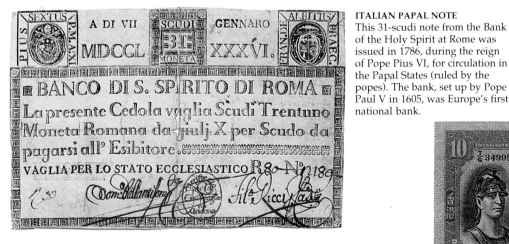

NEW JERSEY "BILL"
When the British government failed to supply its North American colonies with coins, the colonies decided to issue their own paper money called bills (p. 28).

COMMERCIAL BANKNOTE
Commercial banks have played a large part in the growth of the role of paper money. This note was issued in 1954 in Hong Kong by the Chartered Bank, a London-based commercial bank with branches all over the world.

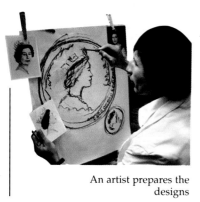
An artist prepares the
designs

How coins are made

A COIN IS MADE by marking a blank piece of metal with designs – a process called "minting." The designs are stamped on to the metal by pressing it between two hard metal surfaces called dies. This is the basic method invented 2,600 years ago to make the first coins; the dies were an anvil (heavy iron block) and punch, and the designs were engraved on the anvil by hand (p. 10). Today the dies are part of a huge, electrically powered machine press. Electrically powered machines are also used to make the "blanks" (unmarked coin-shaped pieces of metal) and to imprint the designs on to the dies. Today's coinmaking techniques are shown here through the production of the 1973 European Economic Community coin at the British Royal Mint in Llantrisant, Wales.

PLASTER MODEL
Once the designs for the coin are approved, an artist makes a large plaster model from them. The fine details of the design are cut into the plaster with metal tools. The more detailed the designs are, the more difficult it is for anybody to forge the coin.

ELECTROTYPE
After the plaster model has been made, a metal version (below) is produced by a complex process called "electrotyping."

Electrotype has a hard nickel face with copper backing

REDUCING MACHINE
A rod on this machine connects a metal point to a drill. The point traces the contours of the electrotype's surface and the drill cuts a smaller version onto a steel punch, or hub.

The reducing machine cuts
this reduction hub

The hub
(left) stamps the design
on this tool, a matrix

Part of a copper bar, called a "pig," of the type used at the Mint

ROLLING MILL
Once the cupro-nickel alloy has been cast into slabs, it is rolled several times until it is thin enough to use.

CUPRO-NICKEL
The 1973 European Economic Community coin was made from an alloy (mixture of metals) called cupro-nickel. Pure copper and nickel are combined to make this alloy. Copper is a cheap metal but is very soft, so a small proportion of nickel is added to harden it. Because cupro-nickel is silver-colored, it can also be used to make coins of higher denominations that used to be made of silver.

Raw nickel reaches the Mint in the form of pellets

Blanks are softened in a special furnace. This process is called "annealing."

A slab of cupro-nickel alloy after the first rolling

Softened blanks are cleaned in acid. This process is called "pickling."

Metal strip with holes after blanks have been cut out

Coin-shaped blanks are cut out by a blanking press

MAKING BLANKS
Once the cupro-nickel strip is the correct thickness, it is passed through a press that stamps the blanks out of it. The remaining strip, full of holes, is melted down to make more strips. The blanks are softened and cleaned, ready for the final act of striking in the coining press.

THE END RESULT
This British 50-pence coin (actual size) was issued in 1973 to commemorate Britain's entry into the European Economic Community. Its strange shape makes it difficult for forgers to copy.

The end result

COINING PRESS
The blanks are finally delivered to the coining press, into which the dies for the front and back of the coin have been fitted. The blank is then squeezed between these dies. It is difficult for anybody to forge coins without having access to this sophisticated machinery.

The matrix (left) stamps this working hub

The working hub (left) is used to make this die

Thin strip cut from roll

How banknotes are made

Making banknotes is a secret and complicated business, because banknote printers have to make sure that notes are as difficult as possible for forgers to copy (pp. 18–19). Some of the less secretive aspects are revealed here through the work of the banknote printers Thomas de la Rue; you can see how they produce a specimen note to show to their customers. Four main stages are involved: design, papermaking, ink-mixing, and printing. The printing is done by three separate processes: lithography, intaglio, and letterpress. The materials created for each of these stages and processes are different for every banknote design used.

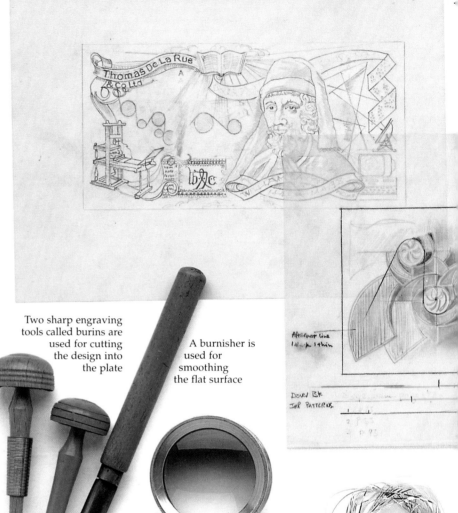

Two sharp engraving tools called burins are used for cutting the design into the plate

A burnisher is used for smoothing the flat surface

MAGNIFYING GLASS
The engraver needs a magnifying glass to work on the tiny details of the design that make it hard for a forger to copy the note.

SECURITY THREAD
This plastic thread is enclosed in the paper as it is made – one of the most difficult features for forgers to copy accurately. At one time these threads were made from metal.

INTAGLIO PRINTING PLATE
The main features of the design are printed from a steel intaglio plate. The features are hand-engraved onto the plate in reverse, using sharp tools. Only the engraved area on the plate is inked, leaving the flat surface clean.

INTAGLIO PROOF
This is a sample printing from the intaglio plate. Intense pressure during printing causes the ink to be drawn out of the engraved areas and to stand slightly raised on the paper, so that it can be felt with your fingers. Some banks use this form of printing to add identification marks for the blind (pp. 34–35).

FIRST SKETCHES

An artist draws sketches for the proposed note. This sketch (left) shows the position of the main features, and the sketch below shows details of the colored background. When the designs are approved, preparation for printing begins.

Blue sheet

Yellow sheet

Red sheet

Sheet showing combined images

LITHOGRAPHY PROOFS

The background design is printed by a system called offset lithography. The different colored inks (eight for this note) are separated into three groups: blues, reds, and yellows. One printing plate is created for each group. The ink on each plate is transferred to a single rubber-covered cylinder that prints the combined image. The trial sheets above show the image from each plate separately, and the combined images as they appear on the printed note.

PAPERMAKING

Banknotes have to be tough, so they are printed on special paper made from cotton fibers. Often a watermark and security thread are included to deter forgery. This picture shows Portals Paper Mill, England, as it was in 1854.

INKS

These eight inks have been mixed from 22 colors to give the exact combination of colors needed for this note. They include invisible secret security features as yet another measure to make forgery difficult, and are only used for printing banknotes and other documents of value.

NUMBERING MACHINE

The final printing process is the traditional letterpress method, using a numbering machine to print a different serial number on each note. The numbers cannot be included in the intaglio or lithography plates because they change for each note. Signatures, which also change regularly, may be printed by this method.

THE END RESULT

Specimens like this note will be used by Thomas de la Rue to show their customers the latest security features developed to protect notes from being forged. They will be shown to banks in countries as far apart as New Zealand, Nepal, Botswana, and Peru, as well as to banks in the United Kingdom, the Channel Islands, and Europe.

THOMAS DE LA RUE
AND COMPANY LIMITED
1422 WILLIAM CAXTON 1491

PROOF NO. 398 D/5

GOLD
GREEN

Forgeries and fakes

FORGERY, THE ART OF MAKING FALSE MONEY, has always been considered a very serious crime. In the past, punishments for forgery included being deported, having your hands cut off, and being executed! However, driven on by the profit to be made by turning inexpensive pieces of metal or paper into something of value, forgers continue to break the law, although these days the punishment is more likely to be a large fine or imprisonment. Not only do forgers harm the individuals taken in by their deceit, they also cheat the state by whose authority money is issued. Despite all the devices adopted by coinmakers (pp. 14–15) and banknote printers (pp. 16–17) to make forgeries very difficult, there are still plenty of forgers prepared to overcome these difficulties, take the risks, and, if caught, face the consequences!

Imprisonment is the most common form of punishment for forgers caught in the act today, but heavy fines are also imposed.

PLATED FORGERIES
These copies of gold Greek coins were made from gold-plated copper. They were recognized as forgeries when the plating cracked to reveal the green copper underneath.

Silver case

Tin disk

TIN DOLLAR
This Chinese forgery of a Mexican silver dollar, found in Shanghai in the 1930s, was made by enclosing a tin disk in a thin silver case.

Round half-crown coin cut to the shape of a 50-pence piece

Genuine coin

Lead cast

COPIES
The two copies of a British 50-pence were meant to deceive those not familiar with the new coin. One is made from lead, the other is cut from an old, round coin.

Nonexistent bank

NONEXISTENT BANK
When Italy was short of small change during the 1970s (p. 37), some Italian banks made small-change notes. An enterprising forger printed his own notes, but in the name of a bank that did not exist!

HANDRAWN FORGERY
All the details on this false Swedish 10-daler banknote of 1868 were copied by hand. This was undoubtedly a time-consuming but presumably profitable task for the forger!

18

SPOT THE DIFFERENCES

The first note is a forgery of the 1835 Bank of Rome note on the far right (both reduced). The forger copied most of the details (including the words at the bottom that say "the law punishes forgers"), but his mistakes enabled his crime to be detected. How many can you spot?

Checking change

In order to protect themselves from losing money by receiving a forged coin or note, traders have always been very careful to check all the money paid to them. When money was in the form of gold and silver coins, the best precaution was to check that the gold or silver was of good quality, and that each coin contained the full weight of precious metal. There were various ways of doing this.

THE HANGMAN'S NOOSE

This cartoon (reduced) is in the form of a Bank of England note. It criticizes the severe punishment for using forged notes, and shows Britannia (the bank's emblem) eating children, and the pound sign as a hangman's noose.

Greek silver coin, 5th century

Punch to test whether coin was plated

Portuguese Indian coin, 1688

CHECKED COINS

In order to be sure that a coin was not plated, traders would cut into the surface, as has been done on this Greek coin. The Indian coin has been checked with small engraved punches.

TOUCHSTONE AND NEEDLES

To check the quality of a gold coin, a trader would mark the black touchstone with the equivalent gold carat touch needle (above), and then compare that mark with the mark the coin left. The streaks here (left to right) were made with 24-, 9-, 12-, 15-, 18-, and 22-carat gold.

24-carat gold coin

COIN BALANCE AND WEIGHTS

This British balance scale was used in the 18th century to weigh gold coins. The brass weights above are from 17th-century Belgium, and are varied so that foreign gold coins imported into the area from the Netherlands, France, England, Scotland, Italy, Portugal, Hungary, and Morocco could be weighed.

A plated coin of the right weight would be too thick to go through this slot

Money and trade

MONEY IS the basis for trade, whether it takes place in the village shop or on the international commodities (products) market. Money, the "medium of exchange," enables both buyer and seller to trade what they have in order to get what they want. In the days when money took the form of precious metals such as gold and silver, heavy chests of coins were shipped around the world in trade! However, sometimes the money itself stayed still, while the ownership of it was transferred by pieces of paper called bills of exchange. Today, money rarely moves in trade. Although bills of exchange are still in use, most international payments are made by telephone and computer (pp. 58–59).

OWLS EVERYWHERE!
The silver coins of Athens (right) were known as "owls" because of their design; the Little Owl was the special bird of the goddess Athena. Athens was the richest city of Ancient Greece, and traded throughout the world with its silver coins. The design was so popular that many countries issued coins with a similar design, as you can see from this map.

Turkey

Italy

Iraq

Athens

Palestine

Iran

Egypt

Southern Arabia

DUTCH TRADERS' MANUAL
During the 16th century, so many foreign coins were handled by Dutch merchants that they used handbooks to identify current coins from other lands and to figure out their value. The one here was published in Antwerp in 1580. These pages show Scandinavian silver dalers (pp. 42–45).

Daelder van Denemercke.

Daelder van Sweden.

Daelder van Sweden.

Daelder van Sweden.

Daelder van Denemercke.

Daelder van Sweden.

BARTER
Today, international trade is often carried out without money; tractors are swapped for jam, and grain for oil. This form of trade, known as "barter," has a long history; the earliest record of it comes from ancient Egypt, 4,500 years ago. The main problem with barter is deciding how many pots of jam each tractor is worth!

Canada

Australia

Great Britain

PIECES OF EIGHT
Spanish silver "pieces of eight" (8-reales coins) were popularly known as "dollars." The Spanish empire exported so many of these in trade that they were adopted in many countries as official money, but were stamped or cut for local use. The coins here all came from the Spanish mint in Mexico City. In China, the dollar became the standard form of money until the 1930s (p. 52).

British West Africa

West Indies

China

Chinese gold bar salvaged from the wreck of a merchant ship

CHINESE GOLD
Spanish silver "pieces of eight" were traded with China in exchange for gold. Gold bars like this were shipped back to Europe, where they were made into coins. This bar was found in the wreck of a merchant ship sailing from China to Europe.

DOLLAR NOTE
After the end of Spanish rule in the Americas, the new republics, including Mexico, continued to issue dollars for export to China. This Mexican dollar note was printed for a British trade bank to issue in China.

BILL OF EXCHANGE
Coins are no longer used in international trade, and money is usually paid by telephone messages between bank computers or by written instructions like this bill of exchange. A bill of exchange is a written order signed by one trader instructing a second person, or bank, to pay from his account a specified amount in a specified currency to the other trader by a specified date.

Money in war

ALEXANDER THE GREAT
This silver coin (slightly enlarged) was made by Alexander the Great in 326 B.C. to commemorate his victory over an Indian king. The king is on an elephant.

SIEGE GOLD
During the siege of Athens by the Spartans in 406 B.C., silver owl coins (p. 20) ran out. The Athenians had to melt down golden statues of the goddess of victory to make these coins!

THROUGHOUT HISTORY, money and war seem to have marched along hand in hand. Money plays a large part in the preparations for war, since it pays for the necessary arms and buys the services of mercenaries, professional soldiers who will fight for any country that pays them enough. The hardships of war have led to the issue of new forms of money in cities under siege (cut off and surrounded by the enemy) as well as by governments that have run out of money. The same circumstances have also brought into circulation unofficial forms of money such as cigarettes. Too often money provides the reward for success in war; in the past, soldiers have frequently been recruited on the understanding that they would be paid from the booty captured from the enemy.

SIEGE NOTE
When a Prussian army besieged French revolutionary forces in the German city of Mainz in 1793, the French army issued "emergency" notes for use within the city. These notes were of French denomination.

During the English Civil War (1642–1648), the Cavaliers fought the Roundheads for control of the country

CHARLES I OF ENGLAND
Charles I issued this coin in 1644 at his Oxford mint after the Roundheads, his opponents in Parliament, took over his London mint.

SIEGE SILVER
In 1644, Cavaliers (royalist troops) besieged in Scarborough Castle in northern England cut up silver plates to make coins. The castle and denomination were stamped on each coin.

CONFEDERATE NOTES
In 1864, during the American Civil War, the southern Confederate States financed the war by issuing notes to be repaid in coin two years after the war ended.

Confederate forces, flag flying, storm a Yankee-held fort during the American Civil War

Distortion caused by blow of bullet

BOER WAR BADGES
These patriotic badges show the British Commander-in-Chief, Lord Roberts (top), and one of his officers, Colonel Baden-Powell (below), who issued the Mafeking siege notes. Baden-Powell later founded the Boy Scout movement.

LIFE SAVERS!
During Europe's Thirty Years War (1618–1648), many German soldiers carried a St. George thaler (top left) because they believed it would stop bullets. At the Battle of Culloden, Scotland, an English soldier was saved from death by the copper halfpenny (right), which bears the mark of the bullet it deflected.

Boer coins

BOER WAR MONEY
Emergency issues of money were made by both the Boers (Dutch settlers in South Africa) and the British during the Boer war in South Africa (1899–1902). In 1900, the British, besieged by the Boers at Mafeking, issued notes like the one above. After losing Pretoria (the capital city) and their mint, the Boers retreated and issued gold pound coins from a blacksmith's shop.

WAR BOOTY
This Mexican silver dollar, mounted to be worn as a medal, was part of the booty captured from a German ship by an Australian crew in 1914.

Mount inscribed "Nov 9 1914 HMAS SYDNEY and SMS EMDEN"

REVOLUTIONARY NOTE
A large issue of notes, like the one above for 10 pesos, was made in 1900 by the treasury at the province of Ocana in Colombia, South America, to pay soldiers serving in the revolutionary army of General Urribe.

SMOKE OR SPEND?
At the end of World War II, a shortage of coins and notes in Europe meant that other desirable objects were used as money. Cigarettes, food, and clothing, all in short supply, became acceptable means of payment. Unfortunately, there was no Hammurabi's column (p. 6) to fix a scale of payments.

"FROM FRED TO NELLIE"
A British soldier made this coin into a keepsake for his wife when he left to fight in France during World War I.

DESERT RAT MONEY
Allied troops serving in Libya (North Africa) during World War II were paid in Italian lire notes, the currency of this former Italian colony.

GREEK OCCUPATION MONEY
Italian lire were also used in Greece by the occupying Italian army. On this note, issued in 1944 for use on the Greek island of Rhodes, you can see the Roman twins Romulus and Remus and the wolf that suckled them, as well as pictures of two coins from ancient Rhodes.

The power of money

IT HAS BEEN SAID that the love of money is the root of all evil, and it certainly seems to be for some people; misers love their own money and thieves love other people's! Money has tempted many people into crime, but curiously, money also has the reputation of bringing luck. There are many curious beliefs about the power of money. Since ancient times, coins have been used to drive off demons, to ensure a safe journey after death, to cure the plague, to protect in battle, and to guarantee everlasting love.

The Phoenician god Melqart appears on the front of these silver shekels

KING MIDAS
Perhaps the most famous story of greed is the legend of King Midas, who asked the gods to give him the ability to turn all he touched into gold. It was not a kind gift, as he soon discovered. His pleasure soon turned to pain as food, drink, and finally his favorite daughter also turned to gold!

The root of all evil

Money itself is surely not evil; it is nothing more than a necessary part of everyday life. However, some people are so desperate for money that they rob, cheat, and kill – where there is crime there is often money.

COIN CLIPPINGS
Before the invention of coinmaking machines, coins were not perfectly round. It was easy to trim a little off the edge of silver coins without anyone noticing, and the coins could still be spent. Coils like these, clipped from English coins (late 17th century), were melted down. In London during William III's reign (1689-1702), people were executed for this crime.

BEWARE. . . PIRATES!
Spanish treasure fleets shipping silver "pieces of eight" and gold doubloons from Mexico to Europe were the main target of pirates. Since the pirates had few opportunities to spend their loot, they often buried their treasure, saving it for their "retirement fund."

Keepsake of child who died aged 18 months

MARY RAMSHAW BORN MAY Yᵉ 4 1773 AGED 18 MONTH DIED OCT Yᵉ 10 1774

Hearts and doves symbolizing love

These coins were issued by the Chinese emperor Kangxi. The characters of his name, meaning health and prosperity, appear on the coins

LOVE TOKENS AND KEEPSAKES
In Britain and America, it used to be the custom for engaged couples to exchange coins as pledges of their love (top). Tokens were also made as keepsakes of dead loved ones (center) and transported convicts (bottom left), as well as to celebrate a birth (right).

Wⁱⁱⁱᵐ Culling BORN April 30ᵗʰ 1792

THIRTY PIECES OF SILVER
One of the world's most famous crimes, the betrayal of Jesus by one of his followers, Judas, had its cash reward: 30 pieces of silver. The coins in question are thought to have been silver shekels from the Phoenician city of Tyre. Tyrian shekels were the only silver coins available in quantity in 1st-century Palestine.

ARE YOU A MISER?
Keeping track of your money is a good idea, but if you become so obsessed with it that you will not spend any of it either on yourself or on others, then you have undoubtedly become a victim of the power of money!

Demon-dispelling sword for driving off a fever demon

Red is a lucky color for the Chinese

Corpse hands over his fare to Charon the ferryman

HEALING SWORD AND COINS
This demon-dispelling Chinese coin sword was hung above the bed of a sick person to ward off evil spirits. Sometimes a coin-shaped exorcism charm (top right) was used instead. In Britain, monarchs gave sick subjects a gold coin (center) to help cure them. In Germany, silver medals like the one to the right were thought to protect a person from the plague.

Money myth and magic

It is not difficult to see why money is considered a source of good fortune. Rich people seem to be blessed with plenty of good fortune because they can buy anything they need. However, many cultures believe money has a more magical, spiritual power. Some believe it can ward off evil spirits. The pictures and words on coins often add to their "power" to bring good luck.

"ANY FARES PLEASE?"
According to mythology, the ancient Greeks put an "obol," a silver coin, into the mouth of a corpse to pay Charon the ferryman to take the corpse across the river Styx into Hades. The coin (left) was found in the mouth of a Persian corpse.

This note claims to be an issue of the Bank of Hell

HOLY COINS
Travelers wore the silver coin charm (top left) to gain the protection of St. George, patron saint of horsemen. Indian Muslims carried the name of Mohammed, founder of the Islamic religion, on square silver rupees (top right). The image of the monkey god Hanuman on the silver rupee (right) gave comfort to Hindus.

HELL MONEY
The Chinese send money to their dead ancestors by regularly burning special banknotes like the one here.

HELL BANK NOTE No.A15917248 行銀通冥 No.A15917248 50000000 DOLLARS FIFTY MILLION DOLLARS

The monkey god Hanuman, guardian of those in need

One million dollars!

A STICKY BUSINESS
A Penny Black stamp like the one above could cost anything between $240 and $4,700, depending on its condition. However, a Penny Blue is even more valuable; you could expect to pay between $500 and $9,350 for one of those.

Roman coin of the Emperor Diocletian, (A.D. 284–305)

Queen Anne coin (1703) made from captured Spanish treasure

Ancient Greek coin, (c. 460 B.C.)

RARE COINS
These three coins (actual size) are worth thousands of dollars each. The Roman gold coin (top left), the English gold five-guinea coin of Queen Anne (top right), and the ancient Greek silver 10-drachma coin (bottom) are valuable because they are rare. However, you do not need to be a millionaire to collect coins (pp. 60–61).

IF YOU WERE suddenly to become a millionaire, what would you do with your newly acquired wealth? Would you rush out and spend it all right away? Would you plan carefully what you were going to do with it all – perhaps investing some and saving the rest for the future? Or would you save it all, never spending or giving any of it away? If you were to rush out to the stores to spend it, you might find that it is more difficult than you imagined! Like many young millionaires, you could spend much of it on designer clothes, records, tapes, computers, stereos, and vacations, but you would still have a lot left.

STACKS OF MONEY
There are 10,000 one-hundred dollar bills in this pile – a total of $1 million. The Sultan of Brunei is believed to be the richest man in the world – his fortune is estimated at around $25 billion.

Display board showing latest bid in five currencies

Modern gambling chips

GOING, GOING, GONE!
People can spend a lot of money in an auction room – often much more than they intended to. The bid for the painting in this picture has reached $97,260 – almost one-tenth of the stack of dollars on this page.

MONTE CARLO MADNESS
Some people enjoy gambling with their money. For them, the excitement of playing games of chance to increase their fortune is often an addiction. Even if they lose, they still dream of winning a fortune. Monte Carlo, Monaco, a town in southeastern France, is perhaps the most famous gambling center for the rich. This gambling chip is for one million francs, and would have been used in the 1930s.

The roll of dice can win or lose a fortune

If you are smart, or lucky, at cards, your fortune may grow. If you are not smart, or unlucky, it may disappear altogether!

MIS EN BOUTEILLES AU CHÂTEAU

CHATEAU LAFITE-ROTHSCHILD
1902
APPELLATION PAUILLAC CONTRÔLÉE

FINE WINE?
Buying old wine is a gamble not many people are willing to try. The wine of Château Lafite is famous, and a bottle of 1902 vintage like this would cost around $600 at auction. However, there is a high risk that wine that old will be totally undrinkable, so most collectors prefer to leave the bottle unopened; it seems that they derive enough satisfaction from just looking at the bottle to justify such an expense!

The United States of America

The American bald eagle

THE CURRENCY OF THE UNITED STATES of America, issued by the U.S. Treasury, is made up of dollars and cents. Coins and paper money were first introduced into North America by various European settlers. But Britain did not issue coins or notes for its settlers, or colonists, so instead they used tobacco, shell beads (pp. 8–9), and imported Spanish "pieces of eight" known as "dollars." The colonists also issued their own paper money called "bills." The dollar had already been chosen as the currency of the United States of America before the Declaration of Independence was signed on July 4, l776. The first U.S. dollars were paper – the Continental Currency bills issued from 1775. Silver dollars were issued as well beginning in 1794. Today the U.S. dollar is the most widely used currency in the world.

BRITISH COLONIAL MONEY
The British colonists did not have any British coins. Instead, they used beads and tobacco, and made their own coins and paper money in denominations of pounds, shillings, and pence. These Massachusetts shillings are from 1652; the Pennsylvanian four-pence note is from 1755.

FIRST COINS OF THE UNITED STATES
After a period of planning and experimentation, in 1793 the United States began to issue a regular set of coins based on the dollar. The 1793 copper cent (top right) was followed by the silver dollar in 1794 (top center), and the gold $10 "eagle" in 1795 (top left). The size of the cent was based on the British halfpenny; the dollar, on the Spanish "piece of eight."

Chain on this tin pattern represents the 13 states united against Britain

CONTINENTAL CURRENCY
When the colonists broke with Britain, they financed the Revolutionary War with paper dollars issued by the Continental Congress. In 1776 a silver dollar was planned but never introduced, although tin patterns for it exist, like the one above.

LEAF MONEY
Tobacco leaves were made into bundles and officially used as money in Virginia and Maryland in the 17th and 18th centuries.

ENTER WHO DARES!
Fort Knox in Kentucky has been the site of the United States Gold Bullion Depository since 1938. The gold is stored in concrete and steel vaults inside a bomb-proof building that is protected by guards armed with machine guns.

THREE-DOLLAR BILL
During the 19th century, most of the money used in the United States was in the form of paper dollars. This note was issued in 1837 by a small private bank in Ypsilanti, Michigan.

DEPRESSION BREAD LINE
The Great Depression began when the stock market crashed in 1929 and the value of the dollar fell drastically. By the end of 1931, 4,000 banks had closed. There was massive unemployment, and many people had to rely on charity in order to eat.

GOLD RUSH!
After the discovery of gold in California in 1848, gold dust and nuggets were used as money in the mining camps. When the gold reached San Francisco, the hub of the gold-mining boom, it was made into coins like this $50 piece made in 1852.

Today's money

EISENHOWER DOLLAR
Recent coins have a presidential portrait as their main design: Eisenhower on the dollar (right); Kennedy on the half-dollar; Washington on the quarter; Franklin D. Roosevelt on the dime; Jefferson on the nickel; and Lincoln on the penny.

BICENTENNIAL QUARTER
In 1976, as part of the celebration of the 200th anniversary of American independence, commemorative coins like this one were issued.

25c   10c   5c   1c

FAILED DOLLAR
In 1979, a dollar coin portraying feminist leader Susan B. Anthony was issued. But it was often mistaken for a quarter, and is no longer made. There are now 441 million Susan B. Anthony dollars under lock and key, awaiting their fate!

LAS VEGAS
Dollar coins still survive in the casinos of Las Vegas and Atlantic City, New Jersey, where they are poured into the slots of "one-arm bandit" gambling machines.

Each dollar note has a different presidential portrait as the central design.

See pages 62–63

France

TODAY, FRANCE'S MONEY consists of francs divided into centimes. The oldest known French money is Greek silver coins made in Massilia (Marseilles) almost 2,500 years ago. From the 2nd century B.C., the Gauls (Celtic peoples of ancient France) issued coins that copied Greek designs, but when the Romans conquered the Gauls, they brought their own coins with them. Roman coin designs remained in use until the German Frankish kings, who overthrew the Romans, began to issue silver deniers, the first truly French coins. The franc, first issued as a gold coin in 1360, and as a silver coin in 1577, did not become the main unit of French currency until 1795. Its value has changed many times since then as the result of revolutions and war. The last major change was in 1960, when a new franc was issued worth 100 of the previously used francs.

The Greek goddess Artemis (p. 10)

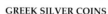

GREEK SILVER COINS
During the 5th century B.C., the Greek colony at Massilia issued small silver coins with various designs, like the small coin at the top with the ram's head. The colony was extremely prosperous, and from about 350 B.C., its silver coins were widely used by the Celtic peoples of Gaul and northern Italy.

PATRON SAINT OF COINMAKERS
St. Eligius, the patron saint of coinmakers and goldsmiths, worked at the Paris mint during the 7th century for the Merovingian kings of Gaul. In this stained-glass panel he is shown using traditional tools for making coins (p. 10).

CELTIC GOLD
The head of the Greek god Apollo on this gold coin (100 B.C.) was copied by the Celts from an earlier Greek coin.

Back

Prow of Roman galley

CELTIC WARRIOR
On this silver coin of the Roman Republic, a lifelike portrait of a Gaulish chief appears on the front and his war chariot appears on the back. The coin was made in about 48 B.C., soon after Julius Caesar conquered Gaul.

Front

ROMAN GAUL COIN
The letters "CI V" on this coin stand for "Colonia Julia Viennensis," which means the "Colony of Julius Caesar at Vienne." Vienne is in the south of France; this coin was made there around 36 B.C.

Louis XIV chose the sun as his emblem because he saw himself as the all-powerful center of the universe

SILVER DENIER AND GROS
Charlemagne (742–814) issued this denier (left). The denier was introduced by his father, Pepin, the first king of France. It was virtually the only denomination used in France until the introduction of the silver gros (right) by King Louis IX in 1266.

PHILIPPE "LE BEL"
Philippe IV, who reigned from 1285–1314, was known as "le Bel," the Fair. This splendid gold coin deserves the same title! Until the time of Philippe, gold coins were scarce.

"LUD" is the abbreviation of "Ludivicus," the Latin form of "Louis"

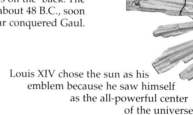

SILVER ECU
From the time of Francis I (1515–1547), portraits of the kings of France appeared on coins. King Louis XIV (the "Sun King") appears on this écu (left). The European Economic Community has recently revived the name ECU (European Currency Unit) for its new common currency unit.

The denomination "sol" was popularly known as "sou"

REVOLUTIONARY PAPER MONEY

From 1790 until 1793, the French Revolution was funded by issues of paper money known as "assignats" (left). Coins like those on the right continued to be issued using the pre-revolutionary denominations, but the designs were changed to reflect the political situation. The franc became the main unit of currency in 1795.

Five-livre coin of Louis XVI issued in 1792, the year before his execution on the guillotine

Royal portrait is replaced by the figures of Hercules, Liberty, and Equality on this five-franc coin of 1795

Napoleon Bonaparte's portrait appeared on coins beginning in 1802, the year he was made Consul of the Republic. He became Emperor in 1804

First Republic, 1792–1804

Second Republic, 1848–1852

Third Republic, 1871–1940

MONEY TO BURN

Because far too many "assignats" were issued, the notes became worthless. In 1796, the printing presses were destroyed, and the notes burned.

FIVE MARIANNES

Since 1793, the main design on French Republican coins has been a female head representing the Republic. The image became popularly known as "Marianne." She is normally shown wearing either the cap of liberty or a wreath. Many different versions have been used; the five here include one from each of the five Republics.

Fourth Republic, 1945–1958

Fifth Republic, 1958–present day

Today's money

Space for watermark _____

LOCAL PAPER MONEY

During World War I, and for a few years after, most small change was issued locally. Both coins and notes, like this 50-centime note of Grenoble, were issued by local trade associations.

COMMEMORATIVE COIN

Commemorative coins are frequently issued for general circulation. This 1988 franc celebrates the 30th anniversary of the election of Charles de Gaulle as President.

10F 5F 2F

1F 50c

20c 10c 5c

31

See pages 62– 63

Germany

This engraving shows a Mint Master weighing out coins in the 14th century

THE MARK, DIVIDED INTO 100 PFENNIGS, is the currency unit of both the Federal Republic in West Germany and the Democratic Republic in East Germany. The mark was introduced as the main unit of currency in 1871 when the German Empire was formed by Wilhelm I, King of Prussia. Before that time the mark was used as a unit of weight and the main currencies were the thaler, the gulden, and the ducat. The pfennig has an even longer history; it was the name used for German silver coins of the 11th century. Before the Empire was established, each German kingdom, state, and city had its own currency system. Similar coin systems existed in the neighboring areas of Poland, Czechoslovakia, Austria, and Switzerland.

ROMAN GOLD
This large gold coin was made at the mint in Trier to reward soldiers serving the Roman emperor, Constantius I. Britannia kneels before him as he is crowned by Victory, a Roman goddess.

Conrad II, King of Saxony (1024–1039)

SILVER PFENNIGS
Early pfennigs, like the one at the top, had French and English designs, but during the 12th century, many original German designs appeared on broader, thinner versions. The coin on the left was issued by Emperor Frederick I (1152–1190), and the coin on the right by Otto I of Brandenburg (1157–1184).

In this 15th-century Swiss drawing, you can see coinmakers minting small silver pfennigs

Coin issued in Rhenish Palatine showing St. John the Baptist

Coin issued in Trier showing St. Peter

Coin issued in Basel showing the Virgin Mary

GOLD GULDEN
Gold coins began to be issued in quantity during the 14th century. They were the same size as Italian florins (p. 36).

Thaler of Count Stephen of Slick, 1519

Thaler of Johan Wilhelm, duke of Saxony, 1569

The arm of God crowns the horse

SILVER THALERS
During the 15th century, the discovery of large silver mines in Joachimsthal in Bohemia (now called Austria) led to the issue of new, large silver coins. These were called Joachimsthalers, or "thalers" for short. The word *dollar* is the English version of this name. The silver from the Bohemian mines was exported throughout western Europe.

The horse leaping over the silver mines is the symbol of Luneburg

Four-thaler coin of Christian Ludwig, duke of Brunswick-Luneburg, 1662

FREDERICK THE GREAT OF PRUSSIA
Frederick, the Philosopher King (1740–1786), reorganized his coin system so that it was based on the thaler and the pfennig. This gold coin struck at Berlin in 1750 was worth 10 thalers.

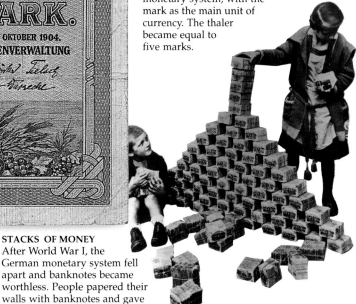

FIVE-MARK NOTE
When Wilhelm I of Prussia became the emperor (kaiser) of Germany in 1871, he restructured the German monetary system, with the mark as the main unit of currency. The thaler became equal to five marks.

STACKS OF MONEY
After World War I, the German monetary system fell apart and banknotes became worthless. People papered their walls with banknotes and gave bundles to children to play with!

Coins made of iron

LOCAL MONEY
During and after World War I, small-change coins and notes were issued by local governments.

ZERO MADNESS
The mark became more and more worthless after World War I, so people needed more marks to buy goods. To keep up with this, banks issued notes with high denominations, like this Cologne 200 million mark note. Bank clerks had many problems dealing with the ever-increasing number of zeros!

Today's money

EAST GERMAN 10-PFENNIG
East and West Germany have used separate currencies since 1948. East German coin design reflects labor and agriculture. The back of this 10-pfennig coin shows a cogged wheel, representing industry, and an ear of corn for agriculture.

Design showing cogged wheel and ear of corn

10pfg 50pfg 1DM 2DM 5DM

33

See pages 62– 63

Netherlands and Belgium

Detail from "The Moneylender and his wife" by the Flemish painter, Quentin Massys

THE MODERN CURRENCIES of the Netherlands and Belgium were established when they became kingdoms. In 1815, the Kingdom of the United Netherlands – which at that time included Belgium– kept its former gulden currency, but reorganized it as a decimal system divided into 100 cents. When the Belgian kingdom became independent from the Netherlands in 1830, it adopted the franc from France, the country that had ruled both countries during the earlier Napoleonic period (1804–1815). A coin system had originally been introduced by the Celts in the 2nd century B.C. It then developed further under Roman, German, French, Spanish, and British influence. In the 13th century, the Netherlands and Belgium were the center of international trade, and many foreign coins circulated there (pp. 20–21).

BELGIAN GOLD
This is an example of the earliest Belgian coins made by a Celtic tribe called the Nervii. These coins have also been found in the Netherlands.

MEROVINGIAN GOLD
The mint of Duurstede is named on the earliest Dutch coins. It is spelled DORESTAT on this gold coin of the Merovingian (ancient Germanic) kings.

Gold lion of Philip le Bon, Duke of Burgundy (1419–1467)

Dutch gold ducat of Rudolph, Bishop of Utrecht (1423–1455)

Belgian silver gros of Adolf, Bishop of Liege (1313–1344)

LOCAL COINS
From the 11th to 16th centuries, many local gold and silver coins were issued in Belgium and the Netherlands. The largest issues were by the Dukes of Burgundy, but local religious leaders, nobles, and towns also issued their own coins.

SIEGE MONEY
These coins are emergency issues of cities involved in the revolt of the Dutch United Provinces against their Spanish rulers, which began in 1568.

Cardboard coin made when Leiden was besieged by the Spanish army (1574)

Lion of Holland countermark stamped on Spanish coins by order of William Prince of Orange in 1573

Bundle of arrows represents the Dutch United Provinces

SPANISH OR FREE?
The mint of the Duchy of Gelderland produced both these Dutch gold coins. The coin on the left was issued by the Spanish king, Philip II, in 1560. The coin on the right was struck by independent Gelderland in the name of the United Provinces in 1616.

Silver coin made by the Spanish governor of Amsterdam while under attack by the Dutch (1578)

THE PORT OF AMSTERDAM
During the 16th century, many wealthy merchants lived in Amsterdam as it was one of the busiest trading cities in the world. The town is cut by some 40 canals, which are crossed by about 400 bridges.

EARL OF LEICESTER
The English Earl of Leicester, acting for Elizabeth I, Queen of England, supported the Dutch revolt against Spain. In 1586, he attempted to reorganize the Dutch coin system.

Isabella and her husband, Archduke Albert of Austria

DOUBLE SOVEREIGN
In 1598, Philip II of Spain handed over his Dutch and Belgian possessions to his daughter Isabella and her husband, Archduke Albert of Austria. This gold coin was made at the Brussels mint in 1618.

This Dutch "daalder" (Dutch version of "dollar") coin copied the Spanish "piece of eight" from Mexico

TRADE AND EMPIRE
A variety of forms of money was made for the Dutch empire established during the 17th century. This silver daalder was made in Amsterdam in 1601 for trade with the Far East, and the copper bar coin was made in Ceylon in 1785. The gulden note was issued by the Javasche Bank in the Dutch East Indies in 1920.

THE ZAIRE RIVER
The only trade route into the Belgian Congo was along the great Zaïre river.

CONGO FRANC
In 1885, the Belgian king became ruler of a part of Central Africa which became known as the Belgian Congo (now called Zaïre). This cupro-nickel franc (1922) was made in Brussels for use in the Congo.

ANTWERP SIEGE COIN
During the Napoleonic Wars, Belgium and the Netherlands were ruled by France. The N on this copper coin stands for Napoleon, whose supporters were besieged in Antwerp in 1814.

French coin

Flemish coin

BILINGUAL COINS
Because Belgium has two official languages, French and Flemish, two separate sets of coins are now issued. Previously, some coins had both languages on the same coin.

BELGIAN WAR MONEY
During World War I, special emergency banknotes were used in occupied Belgium. They could only be exchanged for the official notes of the National Bank of Belgium three months after the end of the war. This one-franc note was issued in 1917.

Leopold I of Belgium

Willem III of the Netherlands

ROYAL GOLD
After the defeat of Napoleon in 1814, both Belgium and the Netherlands were united as the Kingdom of the United Netherlands. In 1830, Belgium became a separate kingdom. Both kingdoms issued coins with royal portraits.

Today's money: Netherlands

Today's money: Belgium

Reproduced with the written permission of the National Bank of Belgium

Raised recognition dots to help blind people identify notes

5gld   1gld   25ct   5ct

20F   10F   5F

See pages 62–63

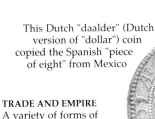

Italy

IN THE MID-19TH CENTURY, after Vittorio Emanuele II became King of Italy, the lire was established as Italy's national currency. The word *lira* comes from the Latin word *libra*, the unit of weight used to set the value of early Roman copper money. Before they used coins, the Romans made payments with cattle and with weighed lumps of copper. During the 3rd century B.C. they got the idea for coins from Greek cities in southern Italy and Sicily, where coins had been in use for over 200 years. Early Roman coins were versions of Greek coins or weighed copper money with Greek designs pressed on them (pp. 10–11). Italian cities such as Pavia, Genoa, Venice, Florence, and Amalfi dominated European trade for centuries. Italian ducats (gold coins) were used and imitated throughout Europe and the Eastern Mediterranean.

In the time of Augustus (27 B.C. – A.D. 14), soldiers of the Roman army were paid 225 denarii (silver coins) a year

GREEK SILVER
Starting in the 6th century B.C., many Greek settlements in southern Italy issued their own coins. This example was minted at Tarento during the 4th century B.C.

I, the Roman numeral 1, showed that this coin represented one pound (libra) of copper

X, the Roman numeral 10, showed that this silver denarius was worth 10 of the copper one-pound coins

EARLY ROMAN MONEY
Weighed cast copper lumps, like the one above, were Rome's first form of money. During the 3rd century, coin-shaped lumps (left) were used instead (pp. 10–11). A silver coin, or denarius, showing the head of the goddess Roma, was issued at the same time.

Silver denarius of Julius Caesar, 44 B.C.

Gold aureus of Augustus, 27 B.C.– A.D. 14

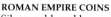

Bronze sestertius of Nero, 54 – A.D. 68

ROMAN EMPIRE COINS
Silver, gold, and bronze coins were issued by most Roman emperors. Their portrait was usually the main design. The emperors often used these coins to make themselves known to their subjects. It was a good way to show people what they looked like, what they did, and what their titles were. Remember, there were no newspapers or television in those days!

BARBARIAN COIN
You can just see the twin founders of Rome – Romulus and Remus – and the wolf who helped look after them on this bronze coin issued by the Ostrogoth (barbarian) conquerors of the city in the 6th century.

ANYONE FOR THE GAMES?
The Colosseum, the most famous monument of the Roman Empire, was pictured on coins in A.D. 80, the year it was completed. It was here that games were held in which gladiators and animals fought to the death to provide "entertainment" for the emperors and citizens.

This 20-"ducat" coin is from the "duchy" of Venice

ARABS AND NORMANS
This gold coin was issued by the Arab rulers of Sicily. The criss-cross pattern on it is made up of Arabic writing. The copper coin was made by the Norman rulers of Naples who fought the Arabs for control of southern Italy during the late 11th century. The Normans won.

DUCAT AND FLORIN
During the 13th century, the Italian cities of Venice and Florence began to issue gold coins called ducats, or sequins, in Venice, and florins in Florence. The large coin on the left is a 20-ducat piece from Venice. The smaller piece is a Florentine florin. The first German gold coins were modeled after the florin (p. 32).

PRINCE AND POPE
Roman Empire coin designs became popular again in Italy in the late 15th century; lifelike portraits of rulers were stamped on the coins. The ruler on the silver coin is Cosimo Medici of Florence (1536–1574), and the gold coin shows Pope Leo X, Medici (1513–1521). The Medici family became very wealthy as merchants and bankers, and were extremely influential in Florence.

Austrian coin

Spanish coin

Sardinian coin

CONTENDING POWERS
A copper coin of the Austrian empress Maria Theresa (1740–1780), a gold coin of Vittorio Amadeo of Savoy, king of Sardinia (1773–1796), and a silver coin of Ferdinand IV, the Spanish king of the Two Sicilies (1759–1825), represent the three main powers that were struggling for control of Italy during the 18th century.

Year 7 of the French Republic

ROMAN "ASSIGNAT" *right*
In 1798, the states ruled by the pope rejected his authority and together formed the Roman Republic. Like the French Republic that inspired it, the Roman Republic also issued "assignats" (p. 31).

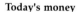

ITALIAN BANKERS
The practice of banking first began in the 14th century in Lombardy, an area in northern Italy. This was the beginning of modern commercial banking as we know it today.

LIRE NOTE *below*
The lira became the national currency of Italy in 1861 when Vittorio Emanuele II became king of Italy. This 30-lire note was issued in 1884 by a Sardinian bank.

Today's money

L.500   L.200

L.100   L.50

1000

POLITICAL COIN
The Fascist emblem (a bundle of sticks and an axe) was the main design on this 1923 two-lire coin of King Vittorio Emanuele III. As a protest, an anti-Fascist user of the coin stamped the Communist emblem of a hammer and sickle on it.

SMALL CHANGE
In the 1970s a shortage of small-denomination coins forced shopkeepers to give telephone tokens and candy as change.

5000 LIRE CINQUEMILA

10000 LIRE DIECIMILA

D'ITALIA   NA 287735 G

KA 409715 F   BANCA D'ITALIA   KA 409715 F

50000 LIRE CINQUANTAMILA

100000

AA 000000 A

37

See pages 62– 63

Spain and Portugal

IN 1492, CHRISTOPHER COLUMBUS set out from Spain to open up a westward route to the East, and found the Americas. Six years later, the Portuguese navigator Vasco da Gama sailed around Africa to India. These two events dramatically changed the history of money. They led to the issue of European-style coins in the Americas, Africa, and eventually Asia, and also brought to Europe vast amounts of gold and silver from those continents. Spain shipped millions of silver "pieces of eight" into Europe and Asia from Mexico, Peru, and Bolivia. Portugal supplied Europe with gold taken from Africa, India, China, and Brazil. Spain's peseta (pta), introduced in 1869, got its name from the popular term for a small silver coin. The modern Portuguese escudo (esc) is a more recent creation; it was first issued in 1915.

Carthaginian coin, Spain, 210 B.C.

Spanish Celtic coin, c. 100 B.C.

Coin of Carthaginian settlement at Salacia in Portugal, c. 100 B.C.

ANCIENT COINS
Greek colonists had introduced coinage into Spain and Portugal by the 4th century B.C. Their main mint was at Emporium (now called Ampurias) in northeast Spain. Later, Carthaginian (p. 54), Celtic, and Roman coins were also issued.

Spanish Roman copper coin from Saragossa, c. 20 A.D.

Spanish and Portuguese galleons were often loaded with treasure

Moorish gold coin

Visigoth gold coin

Coin from Castile, copying a Moorish design

MOORISH GOLD
In 711, an Arab-led Moorish (Muslim) army conquered the Visigoths in Spain and began to issue their own coins. The Islamic designs on Moorish coins were copied on the earliest coins of the Christian kings of Castile and Portugal, who had driven the Moors out of Spain by the 15th century.

Portuguese gold coin

Silver "pieces of eight"

Robinson Crusoe

Gold doubloon

Roman aqueduct of Segovia, the mark of the Segovian mint

NEW WORLDS
The search for gold took Columbus to the Americas, and Vasco da Gama to India. The gold they found was used to make coins like the piece (top left) of Ferdinand and Isabella of Spain (1479–1504), and the piece (top right) of John III of Portugal (1521–1557).

SPANISH EMPIRE
The Spanish conquerors of the Americas were quick to exploit the rich gold sources and silver mines they found in Mexico, Bolivia, and Peru. These crudely made coins, silver "pieces of eight" and gold doubloons, were loaded on to treasure ships bound for Europe. These ships often fell prey to pirates!

"I got all my cargo on shore . . . I found there were three great bags of pieces of eight . . . and in one of them, wrapped up in paper, six doubloons of gold."

PORTUGUESE EMPIRE
Portugal's empire in the Indian Ocean was based on trade. The tin coin (left) was made in 1511 for local use at the port of Malacca in Malaya. In 1693, gold was discovered in Brazil, and was made into coins like the 1725 Portuguese coin (right) in Rio de Janeiro, Brazil. The coins were then exported.

CONQUISTADORS VERSUS INDIANS
Spanish conquistadors fought the Inca and Aztec peoples of America for their supplies of gold and silver.

50-reales coin made in Segovia from Spanish American silver

Original VIII (eight) stamp

MONEY TROUBLES
The flow of silver and gold into Spain made it the richest country in the world, but it wasted the money on war. Prices went up and copper coins had to be revalued. In 1652 this copper coin was revalued from eight maravedis to 12 maravedis.

XII (twelve) stamp revaluing coin

Joseph Napoleon

Ferdinand VII

Duke of Wellington

TWO SPANISH KINGS
In 1808, there were two new kings crowned in Spain: the legitimate heir, Ferdinand VII, and Napoleon's brother, Joseph. A British army, led by the future Duke of Wellington, drove Joseph out. Both kings issued their own coins, but the British army used its own money, including tokens showing Wellington's portrait.

PORTUGUESE WAR NOTE
After the Napoleonic Wars, civil war continued in Portugal. This 1805 note was reissued in 1828 by the usurper, Miguel I.

Today's money: Spain

SPANISH CIVIL WAR
This note was issued by the Spanish Republican government during the Civil War (1936–1939). After the war, coins were issued showing the portrait of General Franco, victorious commander of the anti-Republican forces.

"LIBERTY AND DEMOCRACY"
These words are inscribed on this Portuguese coin celebrating the restoration of democratic government in 1974.

200 ptas   100 ptas   25 ptas

Today's money: Portugal

20 esc   10 esc   2.5 esc

See pages 62– 63

Greece and Turkey

TODAY'S COIN DESIGNS all originate from ancient Greek designs for coins first made in ancient Turkey (pp. 10–11). The ancient Greeks gave coins their distinctive round shape, with designs on both sides. Since then, Greece and Turkey have had many different rulers – Greek, Persian, Roman, Byzantine, Turkish, French, Italian, British, Russian, and German – who have all issued coins of their own. The current money of both countries, the Greek drachma and the Turkish lira, are of fairly recent origin. Use of the drachma, which takes its name from a coin of ancient Greece, began in 1831 when Greece became independent. The lira, first issued as paper money in 1930, took its name from the Turkish pound, or livre.

"AS RICH AS CROESUS"
This saying refers to the wealth of Croesus, king of Lydia (c. 560–547 B.C.). He is thought to have issued the coin above, one of the first gold coins in the world.

ROYAL IMAGES
Greek kings are to be seen on these two silver coins: Philip II of Macedonia (359–336 B.C.) on horseback (above), and Antiochus I of Syria (281–261 B.C.) on a coin from southern Turkey (right).

Coin issued for Mark Antony before the battle of Actium (31 B.C.)

Greek writing was used in the Byzantine Empire (A.D. 476–1453)

BYZANTINE GOLD
The Byzantine emperor Alexius II (1297–1330) issued coins like this one in Constantinople (now Istanbul), Turkey, and Thessalonika, Greece.

FLYING PIG
The design and inscription on this silver coin identify it as a 5th century B.C. issue of the city of Ialysus on the Greek island of Rhodes.

ROMAN COINS
The Romans issued many coins in the parts of their empire now known as Greece and Turkey. The gold coin (above right) is a Greek issue for Mark Antony. The large bronze coin from Turkey features the Roman emperor Caracalla.

SULEIMAN THE MAGNIFICENT
Suleiman, the most powerful of all the Ottoman sultans (1494–1566) issued the gold coin below. His reign was noted for its military power.

Seated warrior is holding a severed head

THE CRUSADES
The small silver coin (top) was issued by a French crusader who ruled as the duke of Athens (1280–1287). The copper coins were made by rival forces fighting for eastern Turkey. The lion's face coin (center) was issued by the Christian Armenian kings of Cilicia, now Lesser Armenia, (1187–1218), and the seated warrior coin (bottom), by the Turkish rulers of Mardin.

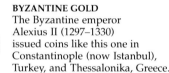

Silver aqche of Thessalonika (Salonika), 1574

Gold altin of Istanbul, 1520

Tughra emblem

Paper kurus of the Ottoman Imperial Bank, 1877

Silver kurus of Istanbul, 1769

THE SULTAN'S MONEY
The Turkish Ottoman sultans ruled both Greece and Turkey. They issued their pictureless coins throughout their empire, which stretched from Algeria to Iraq, and from Hungary to Yemen. The knotted emblem (known as a tughra) on both the large silver coin and the note is the official "signature" of the sultans.

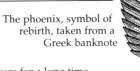

Venetian copper soldo of the 18th century

The phoenix, symbol of rebirth, taken from a Greek banknote

Otto I gold coin

COINS OF CORFU

Corfu and the other Ionian islands were for a long time the only parts of Greece to escape Turkish Ottoman rule. From 1402 until 1797 they were ruled by Venice; they then passed briefly through the hands of France, Russia, Turkey, and France again until 1815, when Britain took control. In 1863, they finally became part of Greece.

Russian copper gazetta, 1801

INDEPENDENT GREECE

In 1828, Greece, the "mother of democracy," achieved independence from Turkish rule. The first coins, like this copper 10-lepton of 1831, were issued by the Greek Republic. In 1831, Greece became a kingdom under Otto I of Bavaria, whose portrait appears on the gold 20-drachma coin.

Greek Republic copper coin

British copper obol, 1819

CORFU CRICKET

During the British occupation of Corfu, the British troops missed their traditional game of cricket, so they built a cricket field in the town of Corfu. Cricket is still played there regularly, but by the Greeks, not the British.

National Bank of Greece one-drachma note, 1885

ISLAND MONEY

The Greek island of Thasos remained under Turkish rule until 1914. This Turkish copper 40-para coin was countermarked by the Greek community in Thasos in 1893.

Today's money: Greece

50dr

20dr

5dr

1dr

NEW COINS, OLD DESIGNS

The second Greek Republic (1925–1935) used ancient Greek coin designs on its new issues. The design of this two-drachma coin is the head of Athena, copied from an ancient coin of Corinth.

TURKISH REPUBLIC

In 1923, Ottoman rule in Turkey had ceased, and it became a republic under the leadership of Kamel Ataturk. His portrait appears on this 100-kurus (one-lira) coin, which was issued in 1934.

Today's money: Turkey

100L   50L   10L   1L

LOCAL GREEK NOTE

During World War II, many locally issued notes were in use. This 5000-drachma note is from Zagora.

41

See pages 62–63

Denmark and Norway

Coin of King Canute (1019–1035) from his mint at Lund

Norwegian penny of Viking King Olaf Kyrre (1067–1093)

SILVER PENNIES
English designs were copied on early Danish and Norwegian silver pennies. An example of the Norwegian coin above was recently found at a Viking settlement in North America.

BEFORE DENMARK AND NORWAY had their own coins, the Vikings introduced French, German, English, and Islamic coins that they had captured as booty or acquired in trade. During the 10th and 11th centuries, the Danish and Norwegian kings began to issue their own coins, with designs copied from English silver pennies. Today, both Denmark and Norway use the krone, divided into 100 øre, as their currency. The same denominations are used in Sweden (pp. 44–45). These three separate currencies were introduced in 1873 as part of a common Scandinavian system. The krone ("crown") had originally been a silver coin with a crown design issued by the kings of Denmark and Norway in the 17th and 18th centuries. The øre was of Swedish origin.

CANUTE RULES THE WAVES!
According to legend, King Canute of Denmark and England tried to prove his power by commanding the tide to stop; he failed. Canute issued English-style pennies for use in both kingdoms.

KING OF DENMARK AND NORWAY
King Christian IV (1588–1648) was king of both Denmark and Norway, but he issued separate coins for each kingdom. The silver coin on the left is Danish, and the one on the right Norwegian.

The letter 'C' is the initial of the king who issued this klippe, Christian V

ROYAL GIFTS
Square coins, called klippe, were often issued in Denmark during the 16th and 17th centuries. Square coins were first used as emergency issues in war, as they were quicker to make than round ones. These two klippe are special coins that were made for the king to give away as presents.

Pillars and globe design copied from a "piece of eight" (p. 21)

The Lapp reindeer herdsmen of northern Norway used reindeer and furs as money

TRADE COINS
This silver coin, copied from a Spanish American "piece of eight," was made in 1777 for the Danish Asiatic Society to use in China. The picture on the small gold coin (1726) shows Christiansborg, a Danish settlement in West Africa where the gold used for the coin came from.

A Viking war ship

MARKS AND SKILLINGS
During the 18th century, the Danish and Norwegian monetary system was based on the mark, which was divided into 16 skillings. This silver krone of 1723 was worth four marks; 64 copper skillings (far right) made a krone.

The lion-with-axe design was used on Norwegian coins. There are four on these pages.

PAPER AND SILVER DALERS

In 1813, the Danish government introduced a currency based on a daler, worth 96 skillings. This daler note was issued in Christiania (the old name for Oslo, Norway) by the Danish Royal Bank of Copenhagen. The daler continued to be used in Norway after the country came under the control of the king of Sweden in 1814. This silver daler was issued in 1823.

No. 517/21a

Een Rigs- bankdaler.

Saa Anfordring indloser Rigsbanken i Kiobenhavn denne Anviisning med 1. Rbdlr., og validerer den imidlertid som Rigsbankpenge efter Fundationen af 5 Januar dens 4 s.

Udstædt efter Rigsbankens Fuldmagt og paa dens Vegne.

Christiania den 6 Jan: 1814

Niemann

Not.

Dolphin and grain symbolize fishing and agriculture

SCANDINAVIAN MONEY

In 1873, a unified currency system was created for Denmark, Norway, and Sweden. The same denominations were issued by each country, but different designs were used. The 20-kroner and 5-øre coins above are from Denmark (top), and Norway (bottom). For Sweden's versions, see p. 45.

PAPER KRONE

During World War I, and for a few years after, local emergency paper money was issued in Denmark. This example was made by the Odense Credit Bank.

ODENSE KREDITBANK

1 KRONE 1

EMERGENCY COINS

During World War II, there was a shortage of copper because it was used to make shell cases. This meant that both Denmark and Norway had to use different metals to make their coins. Norway issued coins made of iron (left), and Denmark issued coins made from aluminum (right) and zinc.

Today's money: Denmark

1kr   25øre

Today's money: Norway

10kr   1kr   50øre

See pages 62– 63

Sweden and Finland

SWEDEN NOT ONLY ISSUED Europe's first paper money, it also issued the biggest coins ever made – copper plate money. These huge rectangular coins could weigh up to 42 lb (19 kg)! Today, Sweden's money is not so strange; it is based on the krona, divided into 100 öre. Until 1809, Finland used Swedish money, since it was ruled by the Swedish crown. However, in that year Finland came under Russian control, and the ruble and kopek were used. Today's markka and penni were also introduced by the Russians.

SWEDISH COPIES
The coin on the left is a copy of an Islamic coin. The penny (right) was made by visiting English coinmakers.

ONE-SIDED COINS
Silver pennies with a design on one side only were made in the 13th century. The M (top) is for King Magnus of Sweden; the A (right) is for Abo, the old name for the Finnish city, Turku.

DALERS, DUCATS, AND ÖRE
In 1534, Gustav I Vasa (1523–1560) introduced Sweden's first silver daler (left). This also circulated in Finland, part of his kingdom. Gustav II Adolf (1611–1632) introduced Sweden's first copper coins, square pieces in denominations of öre (center). Swedish rule extended into Germany, and Gustav II Adolf issued gold ducats for his subjects there. His daughter, Kristina (1634–1654), is shown on the silver daler (right).

Massive man-powered drop hammers were used to stamp the designs on to plate money

PLATE MONEY
Sweden first issued huge copper coins called plate money during Kristina's reign. There were rich copper mines at Avesta and Falun (the copper mountain at Falun is shown on the token above). Plate money was very heavy; the square one-daler piece (right) weighs almost 4 lb (2 kg), so paper money, like this check worth 288 dalers, was used instead.

Anno 1717.
Em Daler Silfwermynt

DALER TOKENS
In 1717, the Swedish government ran out of money because of a costly war with Russia. It issued both paper and small copper dalers instead of plate money. The copper dalers were decorated with pictures of Roman gods. The dalers here show Mercury, Jupiter, Saturn, and Mars.

Paper daler

Copper dalers

Notes were only valid if all three signatures appeared

Russian Imperial two-headed eagle

This design is taken from a Finnish banknote; the name of the Bank of Finland is written in Swedish, Finnish, and Russian

RUSSIAN FINLAND
In 1809, Sweden lost control of Finland to Russia. The Russians introduced into Finland their own rubles and kopeks. The 20-kopek note (right) was issued in 1840. Finland was given its own currency in 1864 when coins called markkaa, divided into 100 penniä, were introduced. The gold coin (above right) is a 20-markkaa piece, and the copper coin below it, a 10-penniä.

COMMON COINS
Sweden's money has been in denominations of kronor and öre since 1873 when, along with Denmark and Norway, it reorganized its currency to form a common system. The öre was already in use in Sweden. This 5-öre coin was issued in 1857; the gold 20 kronor was issued in 1876.

5 KRONOR
5Kr

1Kr

50öre

INDEPENDENT FINLAND
Finland has a different coinage system than the other Scandinavian countries. When it became independent in 1917, it kept the currency system introduced by the Russians.

AR 1840   N°76141

Tjugu Kopek

UTI STORFURSTENDÖMET FINLANDS WÄXEL-DEPOSITIONS-OCH LÅNE-BANK ÅR INSATT EN SUMMA AF TJUGU KOPEK KEISERLIGA RYSKA BANKO-ASSIGNATIONER, HVILKA 20 KOPEK INNEHAFVAREN HÄRAF HAR ATT ÅTERBEKOMMA.

ДВАДЦАТЬ КОПѢЕКЪ.
Kaxi Kymmenä Kopekaa.

20 KOP

Today's money: Sweden

Today's money: Finland

1MK

20p

1p

See pages 62– 63

The United Kingdom

The Royal Mint was located in or near the Tower of London for almost 1,000 years

ALL THE REGIONS of the United Kingdom of Great Britain – England, Scotland, Northern Ireland, Wales, the Isle of Man, and the Channel Islands – now use a monetary system based on the pound sterling divided into 100 pennies. Before 1971, the pound sterling was divided into 240 pennies, 12 of which made a shilling. Different forms of paper money circulate in each region with the exception of England and Wales, which share Bank of England notes. Different coins are issued for the Isle of Man and the Channel Islands of Guernsey and Jersey. The other regions use British coins made by the Royal Mint in Llantrisant, Wales. Celts and Romans introduced coins into Britain, and Britain has since introduced its money throughout the world, largely through trade and war. The pound sterling is still one of the world's strongest currencies.

ROMAN MINT
The Roman mint at London (Londinium) made this bronze coin for the Emperor Maximian. The name of the mint, "LON," is at the bottom of the coin.

SAXON AND VIKING PENNIES
The Anglo-Saxons introduced the silver penny. The coin on the left shows the Saxon king Alfred the Great; Eric Bloodaxe, the Viking King of York, is on the coin on the right.

Silver sixpence

Scottish kings always faced to the side on sterling pennies

Punch marks to test that coin was solid gold (p. 19)

MACHINE-MADE MONEY
In 1566, the silver sixpence of Elizabeth I (above) was the first to be made with a screw-press coining machine like the one in the picture at the Tower mint (above left).

STERLING SILVER PENNIES
King Edward I introduced a new silver penny, the "sterling," in 1279. His new coins were so frequently used in trade that many foreign copies were made of them. These coins are sterlings of Edward I (left), and Robert Bruce, King of Scotland (right).

GROAT AND NOBLE
As trading spread during the 14th century, several new, more valuable coins were made in addition to the standard silver penny. The silver groat (left) was worth four pennies; the gold noble (right), 80 pennies.

18TH-CENTURY SMALL CHANGE
Locally made small change reappeared in the late 18th century when the government failed to issue copper coins. Local traders responded by issuing their own copper tokens. The Welsh druid halfpenny (top) was made by a Welsh copper mining company; the Lady Godiva coin (center) was issued in Coventry.

"The Queen's Head" public house, London

SMALL CHANGE
During the 17th century, a shortage of small change prompted traders and innkeepers to issue brass farthings (quarter penny) and halfpennies.

COPPER HALFPENNY
Britain's first official copper halfpenny of 1672 had the image of Britannia on the back.

LADY GODIVA
According to legend, Lady Godiva rode naked through the streets of Coventry to persuade her husband to lower the heavy taxes. The only person to peek at her as she rode became known as "Peeping Tom."

The thick rim of the 1797 steam press coins earned them the nickname "cartwheels."

GOLD SOVEREIGN
The first British pound coin, worth 240 silver pennies, was introduced by King Henry VII in 1489. This example (c. 1545) was struck at the Southwark mint for King Henry VIII, whose large figure is seen seated on the throne.

GOLD UNITE
A new pound coin was introduced by King James I in 1604. This one (1650) was made during the English Civil War when England was ruled by Parliament after James' son, King Charles I, had been executed.

GOLD "GUINEA"
This machine-made gold pound (1663) depicts King Charles II. The elephant at the bottom shows that it was made with gold from Africa's Guinea Coast.

GOLD SOVEREIGN
A new gold pound coin was issued during King George III's reign (1738–1820). It was called a sovereign, like the first gold pound coin.

PAPER GUINEA
Paper money (pp. 12–13) became popular in Britain during the 18th century. This Scottish guinea note of 1777 was the first to be printed in three colors. By this time, one gold "guinea" was worth one pound one shilling sterling.

Queen Victoria liked to give £5 coins such as this one as a souvenir to her court visitors

The 1849 florin

DECIMAL COINS
The first attempt at decimalization (division into units of 10) was made in 1849 with the introduction of a two-shilling coin, the florin, which was a tenth of a pound. This became a ten-pence coin after full decimalization in 1971.

Today's equivalent 10-pence coin

Today's money

£1 50p 20p 10p

5p 2p 1p

50p   £1   5p
Isle of Man   Jersey   Guernsey

WARTIME SIXPENCE NOTE
The Island of Jersey issued its own locally designed and printed notes during World War II.

See pages 62–63

Canada

Coins and banknotes were first introduced into Canada by British and French settlers, but the native peoples continued to use their own traditional means of payment such as beads and blankets. The settlers preferred to use furs and grain as money, or to make their own token money. The dollars and cents used today were introduced during the 1850s. Variations of the British and French currency systems were used before that but, as in the U.S., the Spanish dollar was the main coin in circulation. The Dominion of Canada, established in 1867, adopted the dollar as its official currency in 1868.

"BEAVER" MONEY
The Hudson Bay (Trading) Company issued its own paper money like this one-shilling note, but the traders used beaver skins as money. It also issued this brass token for one beaver skin.

PROVINCIAL TOKENS
British sterling was the official money of Canada until the 1850s, but most provinces had established their own currency systems based on the Spanish and American dollars. Local tokens were made for small change. In the English-speaking provinces, they were pennies and halfpennies. In French-speaking Quebec (Lower Canada), the tokens they made were called sou.

Nova Scotia penny token, 1824

Upper Canada halfpenny token, 1833

Lower Canada sou token, 1837

Lower Canada two-sou token, 1837

BRITISH COLUMBIAN GOLD

In 1862, this gold 20-dollar piece was made in British Columbia from local gold.

The native Indians traded furs with British and French settlers for more exotic goods

PROVINCIAL COINS

In 1858 the Province of Canada (Ontario and Quebec) introduced an official bronze cent; soon after, similar coins were introduced in the other provinces. The coin on the left is from Prince Edward Island (1871), the coin in the center, from Nova Scotia (1861), and the coin on the right, from Newfoundland (1938). Cents were also issued for New Brunswick.

TEN CANADIAN DOLLARS

This 1906 10-dollar note is from the Montreal office of the Merchants Bank of Canada. The Currency Act of 1868 established the dollar as the currency of the Dominion of Canada.

Totem pole design

Silver 50-cent coin

Bronze one-cent coin

Dollar coin

"Beaver" five-cent coin

DOMINION COINS

The first coins of the Dominion of Canada, silver 50-, 25-, 10-, and 5-cent pieces, were issued in 1870. A bronze cent was also issued starting in 1876. The first dollar coin was not issued until 1935. More recent issues, like the "beaver" five-cent piece, introduced in 1937, have wildlife designs.

Royal Canadian "Mountie"

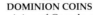

COMMEMORATIVE DOLLARS

The Royal Canadian Mint issues many commemorative coins. These dollars celebrate the centennials of British Columbia, 1958, and the Royal Canadian Mounted Police, 1973.

PLASTIC CHIP

Plastic one-dollar gambling token from Diamond Tooth Gertie's casino in Dawson City, Yukon.

Today's money

$1

25c

10c

5c

1c

Australia and New Zealand

BRITISH POUNDS, SHILLINGS, AND PENCE arrived in Australia and New Zealand with the first British settlers, but because of the many trade ships that went there, Indian, Dutch, Spanish, and Portuguese coins were more common. In 1792, settlers at Sydney Cove found a form of money more to their taste when *The Hope*, an American merchantship, delivered a cargo of rum. This precious liquid circulated as money in New South Wales until it was replaced in 1813 by Spanish American silver dollars (p. 21), which circulated officially until 1829. Today's dollar currencies were introduced by Australia in 1966, and New Zealand in 1967, when both countries adopted a decimal currency system in place of pounds, shillings, and pence.

GOLD!
In 1851, gold was found in Australia. Gold dust was used as money until 1852 when ingots (above) were made in Adelaide, followed by coins (top right). Unofficial "Kangaroo Office" gold coins (center) were made in 1853 at Port Phillip, Melbourne. A mint was established in Sydney in 1853 to make sovereigns (right) and half-sovereigns.

THE GREAT GOLD RUSH
The discovery of gold in Australia prompted many prospectors to search for it.

"HOLEY DOLLAR" AND "DUMP"
From 1813 until 1822, dollars with a hole were the official currency of New South Wales. The silver "dump" cut from the middle was also official money. The dollar was valued at five shillings, and the dump at 15 pence.

Thames Goldfields penny token, 1874

"Advance New Zealand" penny token, 1881

NEW ZEALAND NOTES AND TOKENS
Although British coins were the official currency of New Zealand, most of the money in use during the 19th century was locally issued copper tokens, and notes like this one issued in 1857 by a British commercial bank. More than 140 different tokens like those above were also issued.

BANK OF QUEENSLAND, LIMITED.

TOOWOOMBA

THREE — THREE

№ 1725 — № 1725

I Promise to pay the Bearer on Demand, this Sum of THREE POUNDS *in Cash here, 2nd Jany 1865 Brisbane 2nd Jany 1865*

Batho & Cº London.

FOR THE BANK OF QUEENSLAND, LIMITED.

Ent _____ Accᵗ — A Anderson, MANAGER.

BRISBANE.

Australia's flightless, swift-running bird, the emu

BARTER
When Europeans arrived in Australia and New Zealand, they swapped cloth and metal tools for food with the Aboriginal and Maori peoples.

AUSTRALIAN NOTES AND TOKENS
During the second half of the 19th century, most of the money in Australia was in the form of banknotes and local trade tokens. The Bank of Queensland issued the three-pound note (above) from its Brisbane office in 1865. The copper tokens from Tasmania and Western Australia were struck in Melbourne.

Today's money: New Zealand

AUSTRALIAN COINS
In 1910, the Australians minted their own Australian Commonwealth coins; silver florins (top), shillings (left), sixpences, and threepences. In 1911, bronze pennies (right) and halfpennies were also issued.

NEW ZEALAND COINS
In 1933, New Zealanders began making their own coins. Silver half-crowns, florins (left), shillings (bottom left), sixpences, and threepences were issued. Bronze pennies and halfpennies (below) were made from 1940 on.

50c

20c

1c

Today's money: Australia

$1

50c

20c

This Maori "good luck" ornament (tiki) was featured on the bronze halfpenny from 1940 until 1965

51

See pages 62– 63

China and Japan

The MODERN CURRENCIES of both China and Japan developed from silver dollars (p. 21) introduced by European and American traders. They were exchanged for silk, tea, gold bars, porcelain, and rhubarb! The dollars – called "round coins,"or "yuan" in Chinese and "yen" in Japanese – took over from traditional currencies as the main form of money. China's coinage began in the 6th century B.C. (p. 11), and was later adopted by Japan. In China, silver and gold were used as money only in weighed amounts. The Japanese made coins from the precious metals. Both countries played an important part in the development of paper money (pp. 12–13).

The Great Wall of China stretches for 1,500 miles (2,400 km).

ANCIENT CHINA
Early Chinese coins were made of cast bronze in the shape of tools, like this hoe-shaped coin (left), c. 300 B.C. This shape was inconvenient, so in 221 B.C. the first emperor of China, Qin Shihuangdi, replaced them with round coins with square holes (below). Tool-shaped coins, like this knife-shaped coin (right), were briefly re-issued by emperor Wang Mang (A.D. 7–23).

Inscription gives weight of coin: half an ounce

A Chinese money-changer

THE SHOGUN'S COIN
In 1626, the shogun of Japan introduced new standard bronze coins. The inscription on them meant "generous, ever-lasting money."

Holes for threading coins on strings

BAMBOO MONEY
In 19th-century Shanghai, China, bamboo sticks were used as money instead of the heavy standard coins. This stick was worth 100 coins.

STANDARD COINS
In A.D. 621, the Chinese Tang Dynasty introduced a new standard bronze coin (top left) with a four-character inscription around its square hole. This design was used in China until the last issue in 1912. In A.D. 708, the same type of coin was introduced into Japan (left).

Inscription gives the weight (10 ounces) and the Mint Master's signature

MULTIPLE COIN
During a copper shortage in China, due to the capture of copper-mining areas by rebel forces, "multiple" coins were issued. This one (1854) was worth 1,000 standard coins.

"BIG PIECE" GOLD
This 1860 oban ("big piece") is typical of the gold coins of Japan during the Tokugawa Shogunate (1603–1868). Some Japanese clans issued their own coins, like this lead coin (above) from Kanragori.

The figure on this Taiwan dollar is the Chinese god of long life

CHINESE DOLLARS
Many silver dollars were imported into China. In the 19th century, the Chinese began to make their own; first, unofficial local versions like this Taiwan dollar (1840s), then, starting in 1890, Imperial Dragon dollars.

PAPER DRAGONS
In addition to the silver dollars, the Chinese also used banknotes valued in dollars. This note was issued by the Imperial Bank of Jiangsu Province in 1906.

MEIJI EMPEROR
The Meiji Emperor Mutsuhito reigned in Japan from 1868–1912.

WORKERS OF THE WORLD, UNITE!
So reads the slogan on this Chinese dollar issued by the Communist army in northwest China in 1934.

JAPANESE DOLLAR
The dollar influenced Japan to adopt this denomination for its own coinage. In 1870, the Meiji Emperor replaced the traditional shogun coins with his own "dragon" dollar.

YUAN AND FEN
The Chinese called their dollar "yuan" (the round coin), and their cent "fen" (meaning a hundredth part). This two-fen note was issued by the Chinese People's Bank in 1953.

YEN AND SEN
The Japanese called their dollar "yen" (the round coin), and their cent, "sen" (the name of the traditional standard bronze coin). This ten-sen note of the Meiji emperor was issued in 1872.

Today's money: China

5 fen   2 fen   1 fen   500 yen   10 yen

Today's money: Japan

5 yen

10 fen (left) = 1 jiao (right)

10-fen foreign exchange certificate

53

See pages 62–63

Africa

SOME OF THE EARLIEST RECORDS of the use of money come from Africa (pp. 8–9). The first African coins were issued about 500 B.C. by a Greek colony on the Libyan coast. Coin use soon became widespread from Egypt to Morocco, as Phoenician, local African, Roman, and Byzantine mints were established. From the 8th century onward, Arab and Berber traders established caravan routes across the Sahara Desert to bring West African gold to the Islamic mints of North Africa; from there it was also shipped into Europe to make coins. Farther south, traditional means of payment, such as salt, cattle, cloth, and tools (pp. 8–9), continued to be the only form of money until European traders and settlers introduced coins and banknotes. In some areas, the traditional currencies have survived into the present century.

North

The emblem of Carthage was a horse, shown here as Pegasus

CARTHAGE
This large silver coin was made to pay troops during a war between Carthage (an ancient Tunisian city-state) and Rome (264–241 B.C.). The inscription is in Phoenician.

Arabic writing

BERBER GOLD
The Muwahhid Berber rulers of Morocco brought West African gold north across the Sahara. This Muwahhid coin was made in the 13th century.

FRENCH MOROCCO
This two-franc note was issued for use in the French Protectorate of Morocco during World War II. The French monetary system was used in Morocco from 1910 to 1960.

KISSI PENNY
Until the 1930s, pieces of iron wire, flattened at both ends, were used as money in Liberia and neighboring West African states. They were named after the Kissi people, who made them.

West

PORTUGUESE AFRICA
This copper macuta was issued in Lisbon in 1762 for use in Angola. "Macuta" was the name of the local copper-bar money.

The Nigerian Ibo people preferred to use copper rings as money (p. 9)

LION DOLLAR
The British colony of Sierra Leone was established as a home for freed African slaves. A coinage of silver dollars was made for Sierra Leone in 1791.

LIBERIA
Liberia was also established as a home for freed slaves. Its American founders issued copper cents for the settlement in 1833. The design shows an African greeting freed slaves arriving home.

INDEPENDENCE
The Gold Coast was the first British colony to achieve independence; it became the new nation of Ghana in 1956. This coin shows the founder of the State of Ghana, Kwame Nkrumah.

WEST AFRICAN MONETARY UNION
When the former French West African colonies achieved statehood in 1958, they joined together to issue a common currency that included this 100-franc note.

East

PHARAOH'S GOLD

The design on this coin of the Pharaoh Nectanebo II (359–343 B.C.) is made up from the Egyptian hieroglyphs meaning "good gold."

GREEK EGYPT

Alexander the Great established Greek rule in Egypt in 332 B.C. His successor, Ptolemy I, portrayed Alexander on coins like this one, made in about 310 B.C.

ROMAN EGYPT
After the death of Cleopatra, the Egyptian queen, the Romans ruled Egypt and issued their own coins there. This copper coin was issued by the emperor Nero (A.D. 54–68).

THALERS IN AFRICA
Before World War II, Ethiopian currency was based on imported Austrian silver thalers (p. 32). This note, issued during the reign of Emperor Haile Selassie, is worth two thalers, as is written in both French and Ethiopian.

SWAHILI COIN
This copper coin was issued by the Swahili sultan of Kilwa in Tanzania during the 15th century.

SUDANESE RING MONEY
This gold ring was used to make payments in Sudan during the late 19th century.

FATHER OF THE NATION
Many commemorative coins have been issued in African states to mark their independence. This 1966 gold coin portrays Jomo Kenyatta, "father" of Kenya.

Portuguese Mozambique: gold 2.5 maticaes, 1851

French Madagascar: cut fragments of silver five-franc coin, about 1890

Part of the design from a French Central African banknote

British Mombasa: rupee of the Imperial British East Africa Company (Kenya), 1888

French Madagascar: 10-centimes stamp money, 1916

German East Africa (Tanzania): gold 15 rupees, 1916

South

UNITED NATIONS COIN
This Zambian 50-ngwee coin was issued in 1969 to promote the work of the United Nations Food and Agriculture Organization. The design is an ear of maize, the staple diet of Zambia.

KRUGERRAND
The Republic of South Africa is one of the world's leading producers of gold, much of which is exported in the form of bullion coins known as krugerrands. Each gold krugerrand is made from 1 oz (28 g) of solid gold.

COLONIAL CURRENCIES
France, Germany, Britain, Italy, and Portugal all issued coins and notes for their East African colonies. They did not always introduce their own form of money, but matched the issues to those in use locally. Indian coins were widely used, so in 1888, the British issued a Mombasa rupee for use in Kenya. Rupees were also issued by the Germans in Tanganyika (now part of Tanzania), and by the Italians in Somalia. In Madagascar, the French introduced their own silver coins during the 19th century, but these were cut up by the local people, and the pieces were valued according to their weight.

See pages 62– 63

Looking after money

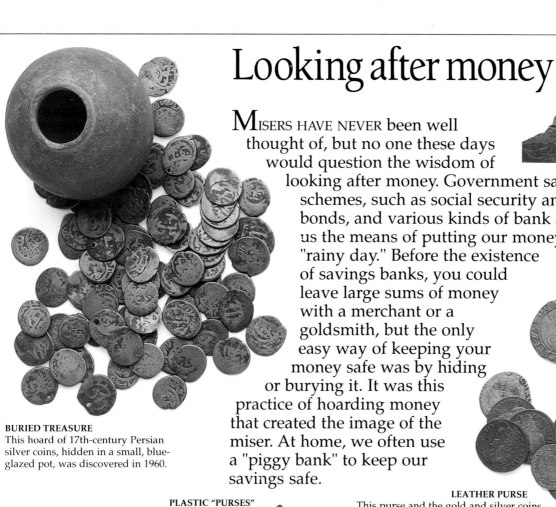

MISERS HAVE NEVER been well thought of, but no one these days would question the wisdom of looking after money. Government saving schemes, such as social security and treasury bonds, and various kinds of bank accounts offer us the means of putting our money away for a "rainy day." Before the existence of savings banks, you could leave large sums of money with a merchant or a goldsmith, but the only easy way of keeping your money safe was by hiding or burying it. It was this practice of hoarding money that created the image of the miser. At home, we often use a "piggy bank" to keep our savings safe.

BURIED TREASURE
This hoard of 17th-century Persian silver coins, hidden in a small, blue-glazed pot, was discovered in 1960.

LEATHER PURSE
This purse and the gold and silver coins it contains were left at a British court in the early 18th century. The money was saved over a long period of time: some of the coins were more than 150 years old.

PLASTIC "PURSES"
Keeping loose change in your pocket can be a nuisance. These two gadgets, each designed to hold British one-pound coins, keep money in place.

Most people these days keep their savings in a bank

Ring for closing the purse

Opening for coins

English oak tree emblem appeared on the back of British pound coins during 1987

Slot for coins

METAL MONEY BOX
Lose the key to this small metal safe and you will never get your money out! The coins go into a self-sealing slot, and the notes into a curved slot on the other end. Serious savers would resist the temptation to spend their savings by leaving the key at the bank. In this way, they could only empty it into their bank savings account.

DRESS PURSE
The 19th-century dress purse above was designed to be carried on a belt, as you can see in this picture. Coins in each end would keep the purse balanced. The opening for the purse was a slit in the middle that was closed by moving the rings toward each end. However, these purses were not pick-pocket proof!

EAGLE AND CHICKS MONEY BOX
Novelty money boxes were very popular in 19th century America. This example is operated by placing a coin in the eagle's beak. A handle pushes the eagle forward to "feed" its chicks, and the coin falls into a slot at their feet.

Handle to push eagle forward

Coins were put in and taken out here

Mid-19th century British pottery piggy bank

MONEY-PIG
The most popular form for money boxes is a piggy bank, but the reason for this preference is not known. In Europe, the earliest examples are 17th-century German piggy banks, but earlier examples have been reported dating from 14th century Indonesia. The piggy banks often have to be broken in order to get the money out.

SOCK PURSE
This woven cotton sock-shaped purse from South America was also made to be worn on a belt. The long end was tucked into the belt and then pulled up to close the hole. When its wearer wanted to take coins out, he pulled it down far enough to open the hole.

TAMMANY BANK
This American novelty money box, made in 1873, has a political message. The seated figure is William "Boss" Tweed, a corrupt American politician who had his headquarters in Tammany Hall, New York. Every time you put a coin in his hand he drops it straight into his pocket!

William "Boss" Tweed sold political favors and defrauded New York City of at least $30 million

Checks and plastic

W<small>E USUALLY THINK OF MONEY</small> as the coins and notes in our pockets, but most of today's money cannot be put in a pocket, or even touched, because it exists only as electronic data held in bank and business computers. Some will be changed into cash before it is used, but most of it will be paid out into another computer. Before computers were invented, money was held in written records, and payments were made by written instructions, usually on printed forms called checks. However, during the last few decades, plastic cards, some with built-in "computers," have begun to replace them.

CHINESE BILL OF EXCHANGE
500 ounces of silver had to be paid out on the order of this bill issued in 1928 by the Yi-qing-xiang Bank of Hankou, central China.

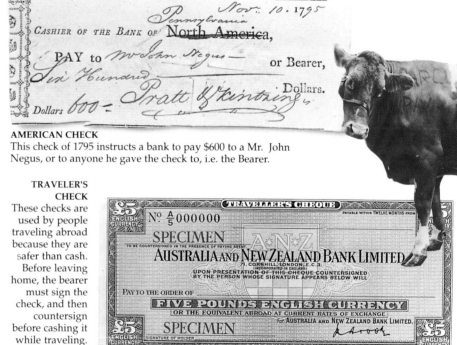

AMERICAN CHECK
This check of 1795 instructs a bank to pay $600 to a Mr. John Negus, or to anyone he gave the check to, i.e. the Bearer.

TRAVELER'S CHECK
These checks are used by people traveling abroad because they are safer than cash. Before leaving home, the bearer must sign the check, and then countersign before cashing it while traveling.

MONEY ORDER
A French sweet shop used this money order to pay a supplier 13 francs, 20 centimes for goods received. The stamp in the corner shows that the five-centimes tax on money orders has been paid.

BARCLAYS

COVENT GARDEN BRANCH,
5 HENRIETTA STREET, LONDON, WC2E 8QA

19

20-23-53
BARCLAYS BANK PLC

Pay

SPECIMEN

or order

£

Cheque No.   Branch No.   Account No.

BARCLAYCARD VISA

VISA ℺ WORLDWIDE SPONSOR 1988 OLYMPIC GAMES

4929

VALID FROM 02

Coutts & Co.
SIGNATURE   EUROCHEQUE ENCASHMENT CARD

MISS CLA
CODE NO.
180004 0

THE BANK OF NEW YORK
ACTION BANKING CARD

53 8

DIANE

Bank of Montreal ⚜ Banque de Montréal
MBB
Multi-Branch Banking
Inter-Service
0012 99

Bank cards

Many stores do not accept checks without a plastic check guarantee card (left)

TELEPHONE CARDS
These cards represent money already paid, the value of which is debited each time the card is used to make a call from a public telephone.

British TELECOM
00019963
KongTelephone
有限公司 電話咭
TELLCARD
Carta di telepagamento
Credito Valtellinese ☑ – Enidata

BANK CARDS
Bank cards can be used to guarantee checks, to draw money from a cash-dispensing machine, and to make payments on purchases.

LIBERTY

Harrods
Harrods Limited Knightsbridge London SW1X 7XL Telephone: 01-730 1234
NOT TRANSFERABLE
1234
AMERICAN EXPRESS

NATIONAL
bank VISA 0850
018
AX

Charge cards

Access
SPECIMEN
5224 999 00035 65
1265 VALID FROM 00/00 UNTIL END 00/00
MR A SPECIMEN
ⓘ INTERBANK

290 597
03/86 CV
CLASSIC

Hologram

In 1970, a contributor to a magazine received his payment in the form of a check written on a cow!

CHARGE CARDS
Charge cards are issued by credit companies and stores. The store records a transaction and the intention of the cardholder to pay; the bill has to be paid later with cash or check. Some charge cards are issued by stores so that their customers do not need to carry lots of money around with them.

KREDITKASSEN
CHRISTIANIA BANK OG KREDITKASSE
527849
Elektronisk
BANK KORT

CB
carte bleue VISA
4979
4979 1234 5678 9123
EXPIRE A FIN ▶ 00/00 CV
MME MONIQUE DUVAL
CLASSIC

Built-in micro-computer that makes and records payments

Cash-dispensing machines like this have shortened bank counter lines

STAR
Union Bank

VISA
SuperSmart Card
AUTHORIZED SIGNATURE
VISA CARD QZ 1 ABC 2 DEF 3 NEXT +
ACCT 2 GHI 4 JKL 5 MNO 6 BACK –
NOTE PRS 7 TUV 8 WXY 9 ÷
NO 0 YES = ×

SMART CARDS
The most recent practical advance in money has been the development of cards with a built-in computer (above). This microscopic computer is enclosed in the card and records each transaction. France's Carte Bleu smart card (above) was the first of these to come out.

MICRO-CHIPS
The computer has revolutionized the use of money so much that large amounts of money today often exist only as electrical charges in chips like these.

MONEY OF THE FUTURE
There is research being done in many countries to improve the use of plastic cards and computers in the handling of money. This example contains its own calculator and keyboard so that it can be asked to make payments in different currencies. The information contained in its chips can also be read by the cardholder. It is not in use yet, but who knows what money of the future will look like – or, indeed, whether we will be able to see it at all!

Collecting coins

THE DESIGNS AND INSCRIPTIONS on coins provide a fascinating view of the world's history. They reveal many things about the emperors, kings, and queens who issued them, as well as the traders and ordinary people who used them. Anyone can make their own collection, and one of the most interesting ways is by theme; collections featuring horses, boats, trees, and birds are shown here. The gold coins are all old and very expensive, but the coins in the plastic tray are all easy to obtain and relatively inexpensive.

SAVED FOR POSTERITY
Many of the coins now owned by collectors were once buried for safety. Luckily for the collectors, their owners were unable, or forgot, to recover them.

A soft toothbrush will not damage your coins

Rubbing alcohol

RUBBING ALCOHOL
The best way to clean coins is to wipe them with cotton balls dipped in rubbing alcohol (ask an adult to help you).

Cotton balls

PAPER ENVELOPES
Because paper envelopes do not contain any acid, which causes corrosion, they will not damage your coins. Another advantage is that you can make notes on the front of them.

A toothpick will get most bits of dirt off without scratching, and a pen cap is good for getting coins out of the tray

LOOKING AFTER YOUR COINS
Because old coins have been handled by lots of people, and perhaps even spent time buried in the ground, they are often very dirty. Clean them with rubbing alcohol, soap, or detergent first, and dry them thoroughly. If the dirt is stubborn, use a soft toothbrush or a piece of soft wood. If that does not work, seek advice from an experienced coin collector. The important thing is to experiment with cleaning coins that do not matter before you start on your star specimens!

A metal point can be used with caution

A magnifying glass is essential for looking at the fine details of coin designs

Sticky fingers have made this coin dirty

What not to do!

Keeping your coins clean and safely stored will make them nicer to look at and safe from corrosion. There are several things you should never do to your coins. Never use metal polish or a wire brush to clean coins – you will clean the designs right off them! Never store your coins in plastic envelopes; they may look nice when they are new, but after a while they get sticky and will ruin your coins. Never put your sticky fingers anywhere near coins, as this makes them dirty.

Never use plastic envelopes; they get sticky and may cause corrosion

A plastic envelope caused the green corrosion on this coin

RECORD YOUR COINS

You can make a catalogue of your own collection. A Japanese collector made this notebook record of his collection of Chinese and Japanese coins in 1812. He drew pictures of each coin and wrote down brief descriptions of them. Two examples of the coins he had are sitting on the book.

This 18th-century red leather tray was owned by a British nobleman

Gold-leaf decoration

A metal or plastic ring will help you hold the paper firmly

You can use rubbing wax instead of a pencil

A soft-leaded pencil will make the best rubbings

COIN RUBBINGS

A useful and fun way to record your coins is by making rubbings of them; you only need a pencil and paper. Put your coin on a firm surface, put the paper over it, hold the paper down, and rub the pencil lead on the paper over the coin. An image of the coin will appear.

Studying coin details can be absorbing!

COIN TRAYS

Plastic or mahogany wood trays are best for storing old precious metal coins. Do not use any other wood, or cardboard, as these will cause corrosion. The coins in the leather tray are the sort of coins that would have been owned by a wealthy person. Leather trays should not be used for storing modern non-precious metal coins, since the leather causes these to corrode. The coins in the plastic tray are more recent, and not very expensive.

Money of the world

Coins and banknotes are the form of money used every day throughout the world, but this does not mean that money is the same everywhere. Each country has its own notes and coins, and usually forbids the use of another country's money within its own territory. This means that travelers and traders must change their money into the local currency. This list gives some examples of the notes and coins now being issued by different countries. They are arranged geographically, from the northwest of each continent to the southeast.

AMERICA

Canada
Dollar [$] (100 Cents)
Notes: 1,000; 500; 100; 50; 20; 10; 5; 2; 1 dollar
Coins: 1 dollar; 25; 10; 5; 1 cent

United States of America
Dollar [$] (100 Cents)
Notes: 1,000; 500; 100; 50; 20; 10; 5; 2; 1 dollar
Coins: 25; 10; 5; 1 cent

Mexico
Peso
Notes: 50,000; 20,000; 10,000; 5,000; 2,000; 1,000; 500 peso
Coins: 500; 200; 100; 50; 20; 10; 5; 1 peso

Cuba
Peso (100 Centavos)
Notes: 100; 50; 20; 10; 5; 3; 1 peso
Coins: 1 peso; 20; 10; 5; 2; 1 centavo

Jamaica
Dollar [$] (100 Cents)
Notes: 100; 20; 10; 5; 2; 1 dollar
Coins: 1 dollar; 50; 25; 20; 10; 5; 1 cent

Ecuador
Sucre [S/]
Notes: 1,000; 500; 100; 50; 20; 10; 5 sucre
Coins: 1 sucre

Peru
Inti (100 Centimos)
Notes: 500; 200; 100; 50; 10; 5; 1 inti
Coins: 1 inti; 50; 10; 5 centimos

Brazil
Cruzado [Cz $] (100 Centavos)
Notes: 5,000; 1,000; 500; 100; 50; 10 cruzado
Coins: 50; 10; 5; 1 cruzado; 50; 20; 10 centavos

Chile
Peso
Notes: 5,000; 1,000; 500; 100 peso
Coins: 100; 50; 10; 5; 1 peso

Argentina
Australes (100 Centavos)
Notes: 100; 50; 10; 5; 1 australes
Coins: 50; 10; 5; 1; 1/2 centavo

EUROPE

Iceland
Króna (100 Aurar)
Notes: 1,000; 500; 100; 50; 10 króna
Coins: 10; 5; 1 króna; 50; 10; 5 aurar

Ireland
Pound/Punt [£] (100 Pence)
Notes: 100; 50; 20; 10; 5; 1 pound
Coins: 50; 20; 10; 5; 2; 1 pence

United Kingdom
Pound [£] (100 Pence)
Notes: 50; 20; 10; 5 pound
Coins: 1 pound; 50; 20; 10; 5; 2; 1 pence
England, Scotland, Northern Ireland, Wales, the Isle of Man, and the Channel Islands now use a monetary system based on the pound sterling divided into 100 pennies (pp. 46–47).

Denmark
Krone (100 Øre)
Notes: 1,000; 500; 100; 50; 20 krone
Coins: 20; 10; 5; 2; 1 krone; 50; 25 øre

Norway
Krone (100 Øre)
Notes: 1,000; 500; 100; 50 krone
Coins: 10; 5; 1 krone; 50; 25 øre
(New 1,000 kr note in 1990. New 500 kr note in 1991)

Sweden
Krona (100 Öre)
Notes: 10,000; 1,000; 500; 100; 50; 10 krona
Coins: 10; 5; 1 krona; 50; 10 öre

Finland
Markka (100 Pennia)
Notes: 1,000; 500; 100; 50; 10 markka
Coins: 10; 5; 1 markka; 50; 20; 10; 5; 1 penni
(New 10 and 50 penniä coins in 1990)

France
Franc [F] (100 Centimes)
Notes: 500; 200; 100; 50; 20 franc
Coins: 10; 5; 2; 1 franc; 50; 20; 10; 5 centimes

Belgium
Franc [BFr]
Notes: 5,000; 1,000; 500; 100 franc
Coins: 50; 20; 10; 5; 1 franc

Luxembourg
Franc [F]
Notes: 5,000; 1,000; 500; 100; 50; 20 franc
Coins: 10; 5; 1 franc
(Belgian franc is also legal tender)

Netherlands
Gulden (100 Cents)
Notes: 1,000; 250; 100; 50; 25; 10; 5 gulden
Coins: 5; 2.5; 1 gulden; 25; 10; 5 cents

German Federal Republic
Deutsch Mark [DM] (100 Pfennigs)
Notes: 1,000; 500; 100; 50; 20; 10 deutsch mark
Coins: 5; 2; 1 mark; 50; 10; 5; 2; 1 pfennig

German Democratic Republic
Mark [M] (100 Pfennigs)
Notes: 500; 100; 50; 20; 10; 5 mark
Coins: 20; 10; 5; 2; 1 mark; 50; 20; 10; 5; 1 pfennig

Switzerland
Frank/Franc (100 Rappen/Centimes)
Notes: 1,000; 500; 100; 50; 20; 10 franken
Coins: 5; 2; 1 frank; 50; 20; 10; 5 rappen

Austria
Schilling [S] (100 Groschen)
Notes: 5,000; 1,000; 500; 100; 50; 20 schilling
Coins: 20; 10; 5; 1 schilling; 50; 10 groschen

Czechoslovakia
Koruna (100 Haléru)
Notes: 1,000; 500; 100; 50; 20; 10 koruna
Coins: 5; 2; 1 koruna; 50; 20; 10; 5 haléru

U.S.S.R.
Ruble (100 Kopeks)
Notes: 100; 50; 25; 10; 5; 3; 1 ruble
Coins: 1 ruble; 50; 20; 15; 10; 5; 3; 2; 1 kopek

Poland
Zloty (100 Groszy)
Notes: 20,000; 10,000; 5,000; 2,000; 1,000; 500; 200; 100; 50 zloty
Coins: 20; 10; 5; 2; 1 zloty; 50; 20; 10 groszy

Portugal
Escudo (100 Centavos)
Notes: 5,000; 1,000; 500; 100 escudo
Coins: 50; 25; 20; 10; 5; 2.5; 1 escudo; 50 centavos

Spain
Peseta
Notes: 5,000; 2,000; 1,000; 500; 200; 100 peseta
Coins: 200; 100; 50; 25;10; 5; 2; 1 peseta

Italy
Lira [L]
Notes: 100,000; 50,000; 20,000; 10,000; 5,000; 2,000; 1,000 lira
Coins: 500; 200; 100; 50; 20; 10 lira

Yugoslavia
Dinar
Notes: 20,000; 10,000; 5,000; 1,000; 500; 100; 50; 20; 10; 5 dinar
Coins: 100; 50; 20; 10; 5; 2; 1 dinar

Hungary
Forint (100 Fillér)
Notes: 1,000; 500; 100; 50; 20; 10 forint
Coins: 20; 10; 5; 2; 1 forint; 50; 20; 10 fillér

Greece
Drachma (100 Lepta)
Notes: 5,000; 1,000; 500; 100; 50 drachma
Coins: 50; 20; 10; 5; 2; 1 drachma: 50 lepton

Cyprus
Pound [£] (100 Cents)
Notes: 10; 5; 1 pound; 50 cents
Coins: 20; 10; 5; 2; 1; 1/2 cent

AFRICA

Morocco
Dirham [DH] (100 Centimes)
Notes: 100; 50; 10; 5 dirham
Coins: 5; 1 dirham; 50; 20; 10; 5 centimes

Algeria
Dinar [DA] (100 Centimes)
Notes: 200; 100; 50; 20; 10 dinar
Coins: 10; 5; 1 dinar; 50; 10; 5 centimes

Egypt
Pound [E£] (100 Piasters)
Notes: 100; 50; 20; 10; 5; 1 pound; 50; 25 piasters
Coins: 5; 1 pound; 20; 10; 5; 2; 1 piaster

Sudan
Pound [£S] (100 Piasters; 1,000 Millièmes)
Notes: 50; 20; 10; 5; 1 pound; 50; 25 piasters
Coins: 50; 10; 5; 2 piasters; 10; 5; 2; 1 millième

Ethiopia
Birr (100 Cents)
Notes: 100; 50; 10; 5; 1 birr
Coins: 50; 25; 10; 5; 1 cent

Nigeria
Naira (100 Kobo)
Notes: 20; 10; 5; 1 naira; 50 kobo
Coins: 25; 10; 5; 1; 1/2 kobo

Kenya
Shilling [Sh] (100 Cents)
Notes: 200; 100; 50; 20; 10 shilling
Coins: 5; 1 shilling; 50; 10; 5 cents

Zambia
Kwacha [K] (100 Ngwee)
Notes: 20; 10; 5; 2; 1 kwacha
Coins: 50; 20; 10; 5; 2; 1 ngwee

Botswana
Pula (100 Thebe)
Notes: 20; 10; 5; 2; 1 pula
Coins: 1 pula; 50; 25; 10; 5; 2; 1 thebe

Zimbabwe
Dollar [Z$] (100 Cents)
Notes: 20; 10; 5; 2; 1 dollar
Coins: 1 dollar; 50; 20; 10; 5; 1 cent

South Africa
Rand [R] (100 Cents)
Notes: 50; 20; 10; 5 rand
Coins: 2; 1 rand; 50; 20; 10; 5; 2; 1 cent

ASIA

Turkey
Lira [TL]
Notes: 10,000; 5,000; 1,000; 500; 100; 50 lira
Coins: 100; 50; 25; 20; 10; 5; 1 lira

Israel
New Shekel (100 Agorot)
Notes: 100; 50; 10; 5; 1 new shekel
Coins: 1 new shekel: 50; 10; 5; 1; 1/2 agorot

Iraq
Dinar (1,000 Fils)
Notes: 10; 5; 1; 1/2; 1/4 dinar
Coins: 100; 50; 25;10; 5; 1 fils

Saudi Arabia
Riyal (100 Halalah)
Notes: 500; 100; 50; 10; 5; 1 riyal
Coins: 100; 50; 25; 10; 5; 1 halalah

Iran
Rial (100 Dinars)
Notes: 10,000; 5,000; 2,000; 1,000; 500; 200; 100 rial
Coins: 50; 20; 10; 5; 2; 1 rial: 50 dinar

Pakistan
Rupee [Rs] (100 Paisa)
Notes: 500; 100; 50; 10; 5; 2; 1 rupee
Coins: 1 rupee; 50; 25; 10; 5; 1 paisa

India
Rupee [Rs] (100 Paise)
Notes: 1,000; 500; 100; 50; 20; 10; 5; 2; 1 rupee
Coins: 2; 1 rupee; 50; 25; 20 paise

Sri Lanka
Rupee [Rs] (100 Cents)
Notes: 1,000; 500; 100; 50; 20; 10; 5; 2 rupee
Coins: 5; 2; 1 rupee: 50; 25; 10; 5; 2; 1 cent

China
Yuan (10 Jiao; 100 Fen)
Notes: 10; 5; 2; 1 yuan; 5; 2; 1 jiao; (Foreign exchange notes also used)
Coins: 1 yuan; 5; 2; 1 jiao; 5; 2; 1 fen

Bangladesh
Taka (100 Poisha)
Notes: 500; 100; 50; 20; 10; 1 taka
Coins: 1 taka; 50; 25; 10; 5; 1 poisha

Burma
Kyat (100 Pyas)
Notes: 90; 45; 15; 10; 5; 1 kyat
Coins: 1 kyat; 50; 25; 10; 5; 1 pyas

Thailand
Baht (100 Satangs)
Notes: 500; 100; 50; 20; 10; 5 baht
Coins: 5; 2; 1 baht; 50; 25 satang

Japan
Yen [¥]
Notes: 10,000; 5,000; 1,000; 500 yen
Coins: 500; 100; 50; 10; 5 yen

Singapore
Dollar [$] (100 Cents)
Notes: 10,000; 1,000; 500; 100; 50; 20; 10; 5; 1 dollar
Coins: 1 dollar; 50; 20; 10; 5; 1 cent

OCEANIA AND AUSTRALASIA

Australia
Dollar [$] (100 Cents)
Notes: 100; 50; 20; 10; 5; 2 dollar
Coins: 2; 1 dollar; 50; 20; 10; 5; 2; 1 cent

Papua New Guinea
Kina (100 Tooa)
Notes: 20; 10; 5; 2 kina
Coins: 1 kina; 20; 10; 5; 2; 1 tooa

Fiji
Dollar [$] (100 Cents)
Notes: 20; 10; 5; 2; 1 dollar
Coins: 20; 10; 5; 2; 1 cent

New Zealand
Dollar [$] (100 Cents)
Notes: 100; 50; 20; 10; 5; 2; 1 dollar
Coins: 50; 20; 10; 5; 2; 1 cent
(New $1 and $2 coins to replace notes in 1990)

Index

Acknowledgements

Dorling Kindersley would like to thank:
Thomas Keenes for additional design assistance; Peter Hayman, (pp. 56–57), Karl Shone (pp. 26–27), Kate Warren (pp. 8–9) for special photography; the staff of the British Musem who helped, particularly Virginia Hewitt, Sue Crundell, Janet Larkin and Keith Howes of the Coins and Medals Department, and Steve Dodd of the Photographic Department; The Museum of Mankind; The Royal Mint; The National Westminster Bank; Pollock's Toy Museum; Thomas de la Rue & Co; The National Philatelic Society; The Hungarian International Bank; G. Smith & Sons; Sothebys of London; Dr. Fergus Duncan;

Coin Craft; Kiwi Fruits, London; Barclays Bank Ltd; Robert Tye; Steve Cribb; Bill Barrett; Howard Simmons; Andrew Oddy; Margaret, Lawrence, Dunstan, Althea and Ruth Cribb; Anna and Katie Martin; and Jane Parker for the index.

Picture credits
(t=top, b=bottom, m=middle, l=left, r=right)
Aldus Archive: 22bl, 37tr, 51m
Ancient Art & Architecture Collection: 6bm
The British Library: 60t
The British Museum: 7tl, 17, 40m, 46m, 60b
Burgerbibliothek, Bern: 32m
J. Allan Cash Photolibrary: 8br, 36mr, 56ml

Dennis R. Cooper: 30t
E.T. Archive: 34bl, 52m
Mary Evans Picture Library: 8tl, 22m, 24tl, 24bl, 25t, 25ml, 31r, 35ml, 36tm, 38b, 39tl, 42tl, 46b, 50, 53m, 56tr
Fotomas Index: 21tl
Robert Harding Picture Library: 29bm, 30b, 38tl
Michael Holford: 11mr, 46tl
Hulton-Deutsch: 33tr, 57b
Hutchison Library: 52tl
Mansell Collection: 13m, 40tl, 42bl
National Portrait Gallery, London: 34mr
Peter Newark's Pictures: 28tl, 48, 49
Pollock's Toy Museum, London: 56b
Popperfoto: 29mr
Punch: 58–59m
Louvre/c. Réunion des Musées Nationaux: 34tl
The Royal Mint: 14–15
Spectrum Colour Library: 41l
Worthing Museum & Art Gallery: 57mr
Zefa: 12mr, 27tr, 28bl, 42mr, 59bm

Illustrators:
Thomas Keenes: 10m, 20m, 54t & b, 55t & b
Kathleen McDougall: 12t, 32t

Picture Research:
Kathy Lockley

The objects on the following pages are smaller than their actual size: pp. 6–7; 8–9; 12–13; 14–15; 26–27; 56–57; 58–59; 60–61.

All current banknotes are reproduced at a reduced size, and in some cases in black and white, according to the reproduction regulations of the country concerned.